CROWOOD SPORTS GUIDES
SQUASH
SKILLS · TECHNIQUES · TACTICS

Peter A. Hirst

THE CROWOOD PRESS

First published in 2011 by
The Crowood Press Ltd
Ramsbury, Marlborough
Wiltshire SN8 2HR

www.crowood.com

British Library Cataloguing-in-Publication Data
A catalogue record for this book is available from the British Library.

ISBN 978 1 84797 256 9

Disclaimer
Please note that the author and the publisher of this book are not responsible or liable in any manner whatsoever, for any damage, injury, or adverse outcome of any kind that may result from practising, or applying, the techniques and methods and/or following the instructions described in this publication. Since the exercises and other physical activities described in this book may be too strenuous in nature for some readers to engage in safely, it is essential that a doctor is consulted before undertaking such exercises and activities.

Illustration credits
All images are © Steven Line except the images on page 19 and in Chapters 16 and 17, which are © Derek Fuller. The images on pages 64 and 72 are © Nick Matthew.

Typeset by Bookcraft Ltd, Stroud, Gloucestershire

Printed and bound in Singapore by Craft Print International Ltd

CONTENTS

ACKNOWLEDGEMENTS

The author and publisher would like to offer thanks to all who helped with the production of this book. Thanks to Keir Worth (Head of Performance, England Squash and Racketball) for his input during the inception of the book. Special mention must go to Gary Hearnden for his great contribution to the mental strength section, graphics and the moral support extended to his son Matthew, and to Mike Harris, Squash Coach, whose contribution, help and support have proved invaluable. Thanks also go to Ann Travers and Elysha Ramage (for proof reading); Stafford Murray of the English Institute of Sport (for material on match analysis); Steve Line of SquashPics.com and Derek Fuller of Derek Fuller Photography (for providing the photographs); and to the players that feature in the photographs.

Squash in the shadow of the pyramids.

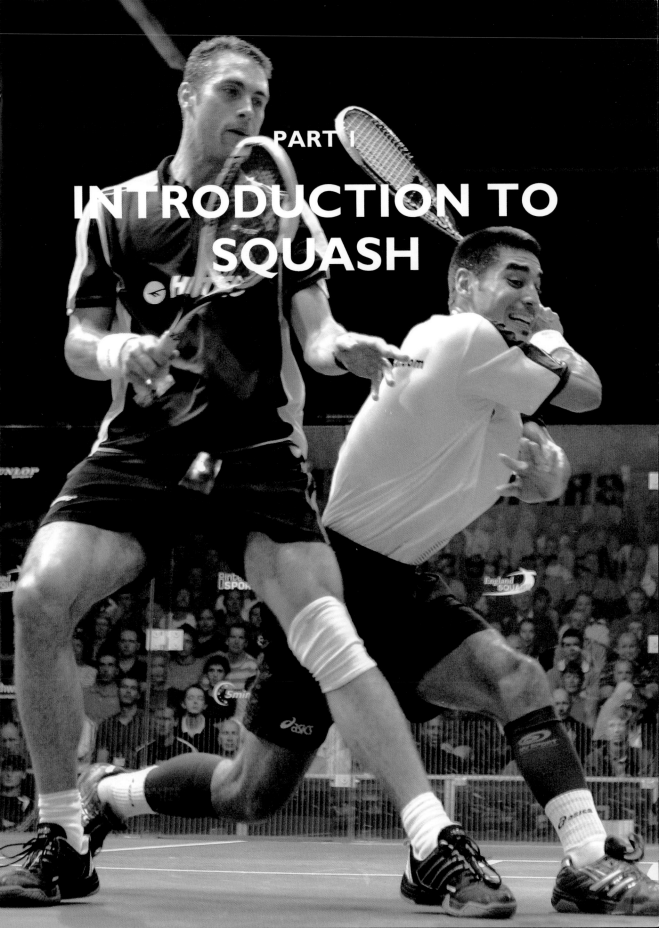

PART I
INTRODUCTION TO SQUASH

CHAPTER 1

THE GAME OF SQUASH

The History of Squash

The earliest records suggest that all racket ball games originated from real or royal tennis. Squash has the same roots, with records of street games in the narrow 'rues' of twelfth-century France. Children would strike the ball with their hands, causing it to bounce against walls, door-ways and roofs; the rules were governed by the local architectural design. Over time the popularity of the game spread to the monasteries and, in the fifteenth century, the Dutch invented the 'racket' and the game became known as 'tennis'. The word 'tennis' comes from the French word 'tenez', which was shouted as a warning before each serve.

Records show that in the early eight-eenth century, inmates of Fleet Prison – a debtors' prison – in London played a version of tennis outside against one or two walls with a hard ball made of wound cloth and an elongated tennis bat. The popular version of this, called 'racquets', spread and was played in alleyways, pubs and schoolyards. Around this time a number of courts were being built, albeit of different dimensions. The first was at the military establishment of Woolwich in London. This was followed fifteen years later by another court at the Marylebone Cricket Club, and a further ten years later seven courts were built at the Prince's Club in London. Racquets was also spread-ing to the colonies, and courts were built in Halifax, Nova Scotia, India, Australia and America.

Similar to racquets was a game called 'fives', which stemmed from a version of handball. It was essentially the same as racquets but used the hand instead of a racket. Fives became popular at public schools, especially the prestigious Eton and Rugby, each with their own version. At the Harrow School in London the younger boys produced a new 'rubber' ball, which was played with shortened rackets at a slower pace. This new version of the game forged a marriage of racquets and fives, which became increasingly popular, and the new sport of 'squash' was born.

The organization of competitions and more opportunities to play led to a rapid increase in the popularity of squash. However, courts had differing dimensions and there was no standardization of rules or equipment. In 1923 the Royal Auto-mobile Club, London, hosted an open meeting of English clubs and formed a 'Squash Rackets Representative Commit-tee' and, in 1928, the Squash Rackets Association was formed to govern squash in Great Britain. The first task of the Asso-ciation was to standardize court dimen-sions and balls.

A further surge in the popularity of squash came after the Second World War. At this time a number of countries developed a culture of squash, which led to the advent of international squash. During this period, Australia emerged as the world force. In 1967 representatives of Australia, Great Britain, Egypt, India, New Zealand, Pakistan and South Africa came together in London and formed the International Squash Rackets Federation (ISRA). Two years later they were joined by the USA and Canada, even though these countries followed a different format of play. In 1992 the ISRA changed its name and became the World Squash Federation (WSF). Since the reign of the WSF, squash has enjoyed its greatest boom, currently sporting a membership of 147 countries with over 185 countries playing. The WSF has led to the acceptance and recognition of squash on the world stage.

The legendary Hashim Kahn taking a well-earned rest.

One of the great battles between Geoff Hunt and Jonah Barrington.

Since its inception, the British Open has been viewed by many as the World Championships, especially before the advent of the professional game. The first British Open winner was Amr Bey of Egypt, arguably the first of many colourful personalities over the years. The year 1951 brought the beginning of the Khan dynasty with the legendary Hashim. This period saw the Khans take twelve successive Opens. Then came the Jonah Barrington and Geoff Hunt mammoth battles of the 1960s and 1970s, with Jonah taking six titles and Geoff seven. Meanwhile Heather McKay of Australia went for a staggering eighteen years without losing a match.

Jahangir Khan, the WSF President since 2002, dominated the world scene for fourteen years before retiring in 1983. During that time he won 555 matches consecutively, winning the British Open ten times and the World Open six times from 1981 to 1985 and again in 1988. In addition to these he won two world amateur titles, making a total of eight world titles. Between 1981 and 1986 he was unbeaten in competitive play. In 1987 he eventually passed on the crown to Jansher Khan, who took his first world title in 1987 at the NEC in Birmingham, England, to start a new reign.

At the turn of the twenty-first century, Australia and England were still the dominating forces in international squash. However, Egypt was developing a presence, with Shabana, Darwish and Ashour leading for the men. The junior players were making a major mark on the rest of the world.

France too was well on the way, with Lincou and Gaultier rapidly becoming a major force in the professional ranks. The Grinham sisters from Australia were making a large impression on the world

FAR LEFT: Heather McKay in her prime.

LEFT: Jahangir Khan at his best.

LEFT: Shabana the great Egyptian.

scene, but all eyes were on Malaysia's Nicol David, who rapidly rose to the top of the tree in the women's game. In the 1990s Sarah Fitz-Gerald of Australia showed dominance, with five World Open titles. Nicol David of Malaysia, currently with four World Open titles, is hot on her heels.

To date, the records show, over a period of many years, world dominance in the men's game, with Pakistan coming out top with a total of twenty-three world team and individual titles. Australia comes a close second with a total of twenty-one world team and individual titles. Third place goes to Egypt, with five titles, and England takes fourth place with five titles. In the women's game, Australia comes out well ahead of the rest of the world with a total of twenty-two world team and individual titles. England is in second place with eight team and individual titles, and Malaysia is third with four individual titles held by Nicol David in 2005, 2006, 2008 and 2009.

BELOW: Sara Fitz-Gerald in full stride.

GETTING STARTED: EQUIPMENT

Clothing

For those just starting squash, shorts and a T-shirt will suffice. If you join a club, smarter clothing is advisable. Normal playing kit comprises shorts and a short-sleeved shirt of a light-weight fabric with a high level of wickability that disperses and transports sweat away from the skin to the fabric surface to allow it to evaporate. A tracksuit or sweat top and pants can be worn during warm-ups, but this would not be appropriate during competition.

Shoes

The recreational player can play in regular trainers, although non-marking shoes are a must as the floor surface is prone to marking. Squash involves many rapid changes in direction. As a result, running shoes are not suitable because the square edges on the soles grip too much during sideways movement, creating an increased risk of injury. Regular players will benefit greatly from purpose-made squash shoes as these provide the necessary support, grip, comfort and protection required for the stringent demands of the game. Serious players must look after their feet meticulously as the feet take a great deal of stress and pounding due to some of the extreme movements required. The constant changes in direction can have a serious adverse effect on the feet, which then progresses over time up through the ankles to the knees, hips and lower back. This can create long-term problems; hence good-quality squash shoes are essential.

Rackets

A good racket is also essential. It must be strong enough to take the odd knock and grazing against the walls of a court. There are many varieties of racket to choose from. They come in different weights and balances and which one you choose is a matter of opinion, preference and of choice.

At one time, rackets were made from laminated wood with a smaller head than is used today. Technology has evolved greatly in recent years and carbon fibre and composite materials are now widely used in racket manufacturing. The slightly larger head of present-day rackets increases the size and range of the 'sweet spot' (the centre of the racquet head where maximum power and control are generated) when striking, which enables the player to extend his range of stroke with additional power and control but using a reduced racket action. These changes mean that players are able to use more deception in their stroke play while making the game considerably faster.

Most rackets weigh between 110g and 180g. The heavier ones are generally good for control and power. Medium-weight rackets are good for beginners and all-round players, while ultra-light rackets are beneficial to get the ball out of back corners and for the quick wristy players who love to play trick shots.

A selection of suitable equipment.

Essential equipment: racket, balls, grips and eyeguards.

grip a try of at least a month before considering building it up with additional grips. When playing with a racket, the degree of tension with which a player holds the racket determines the degree of feel transmitted through the racket to the hand. This, in turn, affects touch, control and accuracy. Gripping the racket tightly creates muscle tension in the forearm. This can lead to tennis elbow, which is essentially tendon damage in the elbow. Try to imagine holding the racket handle with the fingers rather than the hand, keeping the tension to a minimum.

Strings

When you begin playing squash you will not be too concerned about the type of strings used in your racket. However, as you improve, the use of good-quality strings becomes more important. Strings are usually made from nylon arranged in laminated layers, which adds strength and durability. The thickness of the strings ranges from 1.06mm to 1.30mm. A good string will help with overall ball control and increased power. The longevity of the string is affected by its thickness, the tension used and the type of game you play. A thinner gauge of string will give greater response and playability but have a reduced life. Conversely, thicker strings have a longer life but are less responsive. Generally speaking, medium-priced strings of thicker gauge provide good all-round playability, life and value for money. Thicker strings are more resistant but are generally less powerful. Higher-quality strings give better playability, responsiveness and tension stability.

It is important to keep the strings on your racket in good condition. Therefore the racket will need to be re-strung as the strings progressively wear with prolonged use. As a general guide, re-string your racket the same number of times per year as you play per week. For example, if you play twice a week then two re-strings per year are recommended. This is not a hard and fast rule and will vary from player to player depending upon the type of game you play, string type and tension.

To many players, the overall balance of the racket is important. The heavier-headed rackets are favoured for maximum control as the angle of the racket head tends not to be distorted as much as the lighter-headed ones when striking the ball. Broader-throated rackets have a larger string-bed than rackets with a narrow throat. Generally, the larger the string-bed the more forgiving the racket, as a larger surface area would normally mean a larger sweet spot.

The grip size of new rackets tends to be fairly standard. Always give the standard

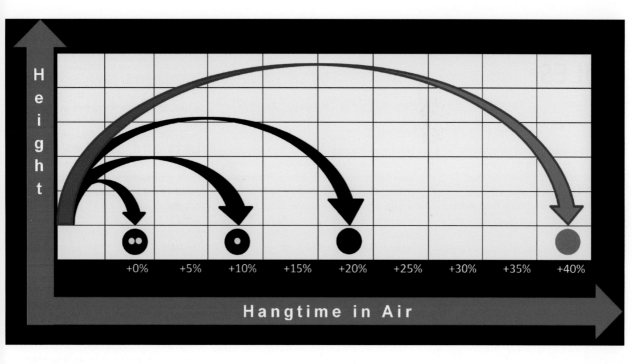

Squash ball height chart (see section on Balls below).

Tension for squash racket strings is normally set at or around 28psi but does vary through choice. Stringing your racket at a higher tension will give more control, whereas a lower tension gives additional power. If the racket is strung at a low tension, the strings will stretch more when it strikes the ball and then snap back to their initial length. This adds power to the shot. If the racket is strung at a higher tension, there is less stretch in the string to provide power. On the other hand, tighter strings remain flatter, so it is easier to control the direction of the ball and to impart spin to the ball.

Balls

Squash balls are made from rubber with a matt surface. They come in differing speeds, ranging from ultra slow for the experts and fast for beginners. After being struck for a period of time, the ball becomes warm due to the air inside expanding; this makes it more bouncy. Top players tend to strike the ball much harder than beginners and this, together with prolonged rallies, makes the ball quite hot – hence they use an ultra slow speed ball to compensate for the changes in speed.

Official slow or ultra slow (pro ball) balls must be used in competitions. England Squash and Racketball (ES&R) approve only Dunlop balls for competition. Clubs play with a range of balls from pro balls, which are used by top players (black with two yellow dot markings), ranging through to quicker balls designed for beginners.

Eye Guards

Eye guards are compulsory for junior squash players and are recommended for all those beginning to play the sport. It is not a dangerous sport, but accidents can happen at every level of the game. Eye guards must comply with the British Standard (BS7930) for Eye Protectors for Racket Sports. They are readily available from most sports retailers.

ADVICE ON BALL TYPE		
Ball type	**Markings**	**Player**
Ultra slow	Black with two yellow dots	High competition level
Slow	Black with one yellow dot	Good club players
Progress	Black no markings	Recreational players
Max	Blue	Beginners

CHAPTER 3

RULES

The basic rules of squash are simple to understand. However, there are some variations at a domestic level. The WSF stipulates universal rules for international squash and in time these will be adopted by individual clubs and counties.

Serving

The right to serve is decided by the spin of a racket or by the toss of a coin. At the beginning of each game and each hand the server has the choice of serving from either service box and alternates for as long as he continues to win points. The ball must be struck so that it travels directly to the front wall between the cut-line and the out-line. This means that on the rebound, unless volleyed, the ball will bounce in the back corner opposite the server's box between the short-line and half-court line. The ball may touch the side and/or the back walls before bouncing. The service is deemed a fault when the server does not have at least one foot in contact with the floor within the service box or if the ball touches the cut-line, the short-line or bounces on the floor before the service line.

Scoring

From a good service the players strike the ball alternately before it has bounced twice. Therefore, without touching the floor the ball must touch any part of the front wall between the 'tin' (the strip at the bottom of the front wall above which every shot must go. The strip is normally made of metal, and produces a hollow sound when hit to indicate to the players and referee when a shot is down) and the out-line. The ball may also strike any other walls before striking the front wall. After playing the ball, the player must make every effort to give the opponent a clear and fair view of the ball and must provide access and room to play the ball direct to any part of the front wall.

A squash match consists of the best of three or five games. Each game is a 'point-a-rally' (PAR) to a score of 11. Should the game be tied at 10–10, a player must win by two clear points. When a player fails to serve or to make a good return the opponent wins the point. When the receiver wins the point they become the server.

A player wins a point when:

* the server fails to make a good service
* the opponent fails to make a good return
* the ball touches the opponent or anything held or worn by the opponent on the way to the front wall
* the ball touches anything outside the court.

At club level the game is controlled by a marker and at higher levels of competition there will also be up to three referees. All appeals are directed to the senior referee and a majority vote is final.

Lets and Strokes

In the interest of safety and fair play, players must endeavour to provide their opponent with a clear view of the ball while in play and allow them to play a shot of their choice directly to any part of the front wall or to either sidewall near the front wall. Should the referee judge that fair sight is impeded or that interference of the striker has taken place they will call 'stop' and a point will be awarded against the offending player. The player can request a 'let' – a replay of the point. This can be denied and a 'stroke' (a point to the person whose shot was obstructed) awarded.

* Should the striker hit the ball which then hits the front wall and touches the opponent on the rebound then a 'Point' is awarded to player A (see diagram 1 opposite).
* Should the striker hit the ball that would reach the front wall but touches the opponent first then a 'Point' is awarded to A (see diagram 2 opposite).
* Should the striker be unable to play the ball as a result of being impeded by the opponent then 'Stroke' is awarded to A (see diagram 3 opposite).
* Should the striker hit the ball that would have struck either side wall first but touches the opponent before it could reach the either side and then the front wall a 'Let' is awarded and the rally re-played (see diagram 4 opposite).

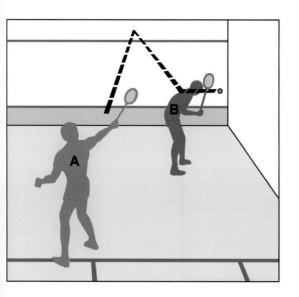

1. Stroke to A.

2. Stroke to A.

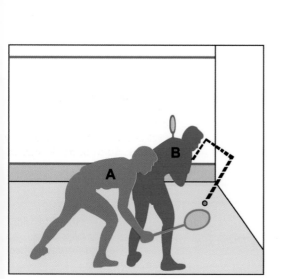

3. Stroke to A.

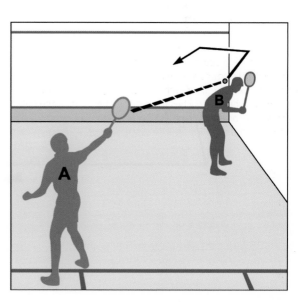

4. Let.

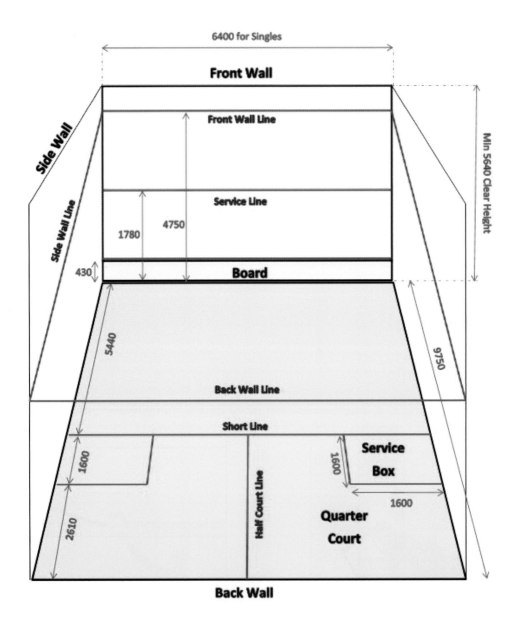

Singles court dimensions. All dimensions are in millimetres. Red lines are 50mm wide.

This could be painful. The striker is impeded from playing a winning shot of choice and could cause a serious injury.

CHAPTER 4

PLAYING THE GAME AND HOW TO GET INVOLVED

Where to Play

Squash is a fantastic sport that caters for a wide range of abilities. It is a great way to get fit and meet new people, while being good value for money compared to many other sports. In England the game is played by over half a million people on a regular basis in approximately two thousand venues on over five thousand courts in schools, members' clubs, universities and local authority sports and leisure centres. All good venues provide the opportunity for coaching, practice and competition across all levels and age groups. In addition, they may provide supplementary facilities such as fitness studios, gyms and swimming pools, which can assist you in developing your squash-specific fitness and in making general improvements in endurance and strength. Activity within good venues is driven by the 'club-pro', who will be able to give sound advice on all aspects of the game, including what type of equipment to buy.

The trend, particularly during the 1990s, for redeveloping courts into gyms appears to have stopped and the game seems to be having somewhat of a renaissance. This has been driven essentially by ES&R and their partnerships with clubs, local authority providers and universities – where squash has always thrived. A strong tradition and culture for squash still exists within many towns and cities and, similar to other so-called 'minority sports', one of the key strengths of the game has been its strong club structure with the commitment and dedication of enthusiastic players, officials and volunteers.

The club structure caters for all the needs of a squash player, from individual play in club leagues to team squash in local leagues and national competition. Many clubs charge a membership fee, which can range from £10 to £100 per month dependent on the venue and the range of facilities and activities provided. Most clubs affiliate to ES&R, Squash Wales, Scottish Squash and Ulster Squash as the national governing bodies for squash in the home countries. This brings a collective knowledge and wealth of experience that provide a wide range of squash opportunities and programmes delivered through the club structures.

Club Structures

All clubs have their own structure and systems, most commonly with a range of activities including: junior training and leagues, internal adult leagues, club nights, ladies' mornings, team training, individual and group coaching, courses and a range of internal championships, including the always prestigious 'Club Championship'. The range of events and opportunities will have different aims – mostly to find the best player – but always to encourage friendly competition, player development and a sense of community and belonging within a club. These social occasions offer everyone the chance to enjoy playing, watching and meeting new people in a pleasant environment.

Most clubs will have several representative teams for men, women and juniors participating in district or countywide leagues, which pitch players against similar opposition in friendly competition. At every level, these matches can stimulate good-natured vocal support from and between each club where strong local rivalries can develop.

Universities

Almost all universities have a sports department and more than seventy in England have squash facilities and programmes that cater for the recreational player through to students' representative in the World Student Games. Some universities, such as the University of Birmingham, have strong links within their community through schools and other local clubs.

There is a thriving competitive squash structure within universities and across higher education, with a multitude of internal and external programmes for players at every level, including intramural activity and internal box leagues. At the highest end of competition, the Universities of Birmingham, Loughborough and Leeds have, over recent years, dominated the national student team and individual competitions. From these competitions a number of professionals have emerged, including English former World Student Champions Chris Ryder and Jenny Tranfield, and the Indian National Champion Saurav Ghosal, ranked twenty-eighth in the world.

Local Authorities

Local authorities are without doubt a significant shareholder of sport in the UK, owning or providing facilities and programmes that serve a multitude of community interests and needs. In

England, thirty-eight per cent of all squash courts are operated by local authorities and are well patronized by social and competitive players of all ages and ability. ES&R have effective partnerships with a number of national local authority providers, which aim to increase participation and opportunities to play, including a number of 'pay and play' schemes. These schemes have been particularly successful in encouraging first timers to become 'beginners' and embark on a variety of courses and events. Furthermore, there has been a further initiative to develop more and better-qualified coaches within local authorities to sustain and stimulate growth in the sport.

County Structures

County associations generally organize and administer inter-club leagues, run county championships, prepare county teams and facilitate a range of development programmes. A key aspect of a county remit is to develop thriving junior county programmes, in addition to providing support and advice to clubs on development issues. County associations have a close relationship with the national governing body (NGB), which seeks to strengthen participation, increase talent pools and reinforce established talent pathways.

Regional Structures

Regional structures are usually an extension of the NGBs for squash, which provide crucial opportunities for player development within a recognized talent pathway. Driven by a NGB, they also provide fantastic opportunities for coaching, competition, coach education and coach development.

The 'back room boys', the rarely seen event organizers. It's always good to see the results of their labours.

National Associations

The NGBs for squash are constituted to provide the national policy for squash, reflective of the continental and world body where competition rules and regulations are set. National bodies are normally the most productive of all squash bodies in the design, administration and organization of a wide range of programmes. These programmes keep squash visible and are made available to member clubs to satisfy the needs of players, coaches, officials and volunteers.

European Squash Federation

The European Squash Federation (ESF) serves as the World Squash Federation's designated regional federation within Europe. It exists primarily to promote the growth and general welfare of squash, to coordinate and manage European competition and to uphold and enforce the rules of the game. The ESF has a key role to play in the development of the sport, by strengthening the relationships between existing member nations and encouraging the membership of new countries.

World Squash Federation

The World Squash Federation (WSF) consists of 147 member National Associations with approximately 185 countries actively playing squash. It works closely with the two player associations – the (men's) Professional Squash Association (PSA) and the Women's International Squash Players Association (WISPA) – to control and coordinate the world calendar for squash. It is responsible for the World Championships for men and women, juniors and masters, and individual and team events. It also encourages the development of squash, not only in countries where it is a new sport, but also where squash is already well established.

CHAPTER 5

THE BIGGER PICTURE

Player Pathways

Squash is a fast-paced sport that provides fun, fitness and highly developed competition structures at all ability levels. It is often introduced through club or county talent identification days or in schools as part of a school sport partnership network linked to club and local authorities. Alternatively, people are often introduced to squash by friends and in 'come and try' sessions through schools, clubs and local authority initiatives as an integral part of a player pathway.

A player or talent pathway is essentially a participant model, usually represented in a linear format, that represents the bigger picture of how a national association endeavours to develop young players; for example, how and where players 'fit' into an incremental structure. This is separate from a talent programme, which defines *how* a specific group of players is developed into elite athletes and *what* services they might receive. A typical pathway includes identified development clubs, county and sub-county squads at junior level, junior regional squads or academies, 'super' regional squads (for example the south or north of England), junior through to youth England squads, transitional squads for talented young professionals and, finally, the elite senior programme, populated by world-class athletes. Each step of the pathway has a requisite selection criteria, or process and progression through the pathway and is dependent on the success of each player as measured by ability. A good talent pathway connects each progressive step seamlessly, giving players the chance to develop to a higher standard or within the aspect of the pathway they currently inhabit.

Two essential components are required at each stage of a talent pathway, *enjoy-*ment and *success*. If squash does not provide the needed level of enjoyment and pleasure then another choice of sport or activity is advised as these are the primary reasons to become involved with squash. Without a sense of *enjoyment* from playing, any success will be short-lived; life-long participation and the health and social benefits of playing are hindered. Without a certain level of *success*, by which is meant the ability to strike a ball, play simple rallies and engage in some games or adapted games, there is unlikely to be any long-term benefit to playing.

For the benefit of the reader, we have included a basic, but comprehensive, linear pathway that will help players and coaches identify their coaching and competitive needs. It is by recognizing your own level that you can enjoy a lifetime of involvement, enjoyment and competition. The comprehensive pathway below represents the incremental development process that allows players to accomplish a standard at which they can play and compete with people of a similar standard. Whereas all the components required to play squash exist and overlap at all the different stages of development, the player's needs subtly change to further refine specific skills. The coaching style and the way that information passes from the coach to the player also change as players develop. Hence, the way that coaches are trained and gain their professional status changes to meet the needs of players within varied training programmes that are designed and delivered to prepare players for competition.

On introduction to squash and when the two components, enjoyment and success, are present, people quickly move on to a *participation* level where they may enjoy club sessions and internal club box leagues, playing with and against people of a similar ability. If enjoyment and some success are present, they may then move on to a *performance* level where a greater level of investment in time and energy is required. At this level, playing three to four times a week, undergoing some additional fitness training and engaging in inter-club matches and some local tournaments is normal. Progression from here is to a *high performance* level where activity will again increase. At this level the player will compete at a regional level with some national activities in events such as training camps and county matches, which lead on to the final, *elite* level. This is the world arena for national and international events, such as the Commonwealth Games or other Continental or World Championships. Through progression at all these levels, the player should feel enjoyment and success.

Player Needs

Players have differing needs at the various stages of development. Whereas the same basic skills are required at all levels of play, the level of ability at each stage of development will differ widely. From examining the exemplar pathway model pictured in the table opposite, it is clear that each stage of development will require a slightly different emphasis that caters for the player's needs at that particular stage of their own development.

Understanding at the Introductory Stage

At this stage, it is important for players to appreciate and understand what they are trying to achieve. In its simplest form, the aim of squash is to strike the ball with the racket so that the ball does not touch the

KEY POINTS OF EMPHASIS

Player pathways	Player needs	Coaching styles	Coaching qualification	Supporting programmes	Competition programmes
Elite	Specific SKILLS and ATTRIBUTES built upon developing strengths and overcoming weaknesses	Support • Medical • Fitness • Management	Master's degree	Specialized	World Team/ Individual European Team/ Individual International Opens
High performance	Tactics • Deployment of a wide range of tactics	Empowerment • To THINK for themselves	UKCC Level 4	National Training Camps	National Championships National league Regional tournaments
Performance	Skill • Advanced rally building • Increased range of strokes • Deception	Direct them to APPLY PRESSURE	UKCC Level 3	Top Player Awards Regional Training Camps County-Coaching	National events Regional tournaments County matches County leagues
Participation	Technical • Basic principles of rallying/accuracy/ pressure	Coach HOW to develop basic techniques and rally building	UKCC Level 2	Development Player Awards Club-Coaching	County leagues Club box leagues
Introductory	Understanding • Outcomes they are trying to achieve	Teach the understanding of WHAT they are trying to achieve	UKCC Level 1	Mini-Squash Club-Coaching School-Coaching	Club box leagues School fun games

floor and will strike the front wall between the red lines, ensuring that your opponent is unable to make a 'good' return. This level of development is currently supported by the ES&R Mini-Squash Awards. Other key skills are encompassed within multi-sport initiatives.

Developing Technical Ability at the Participation Stage

Once a player has achieved a level of success and enjoyment at the introductory stage, his needs change slightly and start to focus upon the development of key techniques, which are underpinned by biomechanical principles of movement.

This stage also includes developing the basic and simple ability of how to rally with a degree of accuracy and how to begin to 'build pressure' on an opponent. This level of development is supported by the ES&R Development Awards, which begin to focus players more intensely upon squash-specific development.

Skill Development at the Performance Stage

Once a player has developed a significant technical competence, the emphasis of their needs alters and the coach will begin to concentrate upon skill development. This will include the ability to:

- build more complex rallies
- execute an increased range of advanced strokes
- apply an increasing degree of pressure upon an opponent
  - by reducing their shot *options*, *time* to recover and play a shot
  - by increasing the *distance* they have to travel around the court.

At this stage of development it is important that players take extra care and attention to build an individual *style* that is unique to each individual. This is when players apply practically the techniques expressed through their personality in the most natural way for them to the best effect in competition.

Developing Greater Tactical Awareness at the High Performance Stage

At the high performance stage, the emphasis of development shifts to the employment and deployment of advanced tactics. There will, of course, be a need to continually refine technique and improve skill levels, but players should be empowered to be able to apply the *right tactics*, at the *right time*.

Further Development at the Elite Stage

At the final stage, elite or world-class players are required to operate in a 'supportive' style and their requirements will include the 'sum of everything' covered to date. Their needs will be individually unique, developing specific advanced skills and attributes to build upon existing strengths and to overcome weaknesses.

Coaching Styles

Linked directly to the varying needs of developing players is the way in which information passes from a coach or helpers to the player *or* how the player learns from watching other players. It is important that players are able to perform all the skills required rather than just have an understanding of them.

Teach

In the first phase the coach teaches or facilitates *learning for understanding*. The player needs to have a clear understanding of what they are trying to achieve when they start learning. This usually can be summed up by the simple question: What do I want to make the ball do? This will involve understanding the trajectory of the ball travelling to the front wall with sufficient pace and power to rebound to a further target in the court. This simple understanding usually comes quickly and

should remain a close focus of attention until it becomes a subconscious action.

Coach

In the second phase the coach encourages the player to develop the technical ability of striking the ball. This is achieved by the coach guiding the player to (1) read the situation on the court, (2) make decisions on what they are trying to make the ball do, (3) coordinate their movements in relation to the position of the ball and (4) strike it with some accuracy. Likely comments and questions from the coach are:

- Try this or that.
- Does that feel better?
- Did you have a better result or outcome?
- What was the effect of …?

Direct

In the third phase the coach directs the player towards combining all the tactics that will apply pressure on their opponent. This includes an increase in the range of shots that they play, integrated with more advanced rallies and the ability to use disguise and deception. In addition, the player must constantly be aware of their opponent's actions and what likely outcomes may occur. Likely questions are:

- When you struck the ball early what advantage did you gain?
- Did you create a possible advantage?
- What could you do next to gain further advantage?

Empower

The role of the coach in the fourth phase is to empower the player to think and act for himself. On the practice court, the coach will instruct on both general and specific tactics, which the player then needs to act upon on the match court. By this stage of development the player will, and should, have a good level of ability,

and in the match situation will often *go with their first instinct* rather than listen to the coach yelling from court side.

Support

During the fifth phase the role of the coach is to support the player, who at this level will be very proficient. A player reaching an elite standard is able to display:

- a good *understanding* of what they are doing
- a mastery of good *technique*
- *skilful* application
- employment and deployment of effective *tactics*.

Coaching and Coaching Education

Coaches and coaching often bring camaraderie and social interaction to squash, which is health enhancing and many would say character building. In the UK we have enjoyed a strong culture of sport, inventing and developing structures for sport in perpetuity. If we genuinely value our culture of sport, in our case squash, we must understand that it is the coaches and helpers who will play a major part in perpetuating this culture for the future sporting nation.

Coaches and good quality coaching are the catalyst for development of players and the game as a whole. They are part of the driving force that facilitates levels of activity within clubs around the world, as well as providing instruction and inspiration to players at every level. Indeed, it is coaches who motivate, encourage and facilitate participation and, without them, most players would fail to fulfil their potential, regardless of their ability. The benefits of receiving coaching are significant, as no matter what standard of player you are, you will benefit from being observed, analysed and advised from someone with an appropriate level of knowledge and understanding. Clearly the more experienced and qualified the coach is, the better

THE UKCC-ENDORSED SQUASH COACHING QUALIFICATIONS

Level of UKCC qualification	What the coach is able to do on completion of the qualification
Level 1	Assist more qualified coaches delivering aspects of a coaching session normally under direct supervision
Level 2	Prepare for, deliver and review coaching sessions
Level 3	Plan, implement, analyse and revise annual coaching programmes
Level 4	Level 4 coach has the vision, values, skills and behaviours to effect change and develop, lead and evaluate a cutting-edge coaching programme, or part of the programme, that results in a positive impact on the participants' behaviour and performance

their ability to help the players they work with. As with other professions, however, some coaches are better than others, and some suit or prefer working with specific age groups or standards. Problems can occur when coaches fail to adhere to a programme of continued professional development (CPD), neglect the needs of a player to further themselves, or fail to remember the key concept that participation is for fun and enjoyment, as well as the need to improve and achieve.

Coaching has continued to emerge as a profession over recent years and Coach Education has consequently developed significantly, especially since the introduction of the UK Coaching Certificate (UKCC) in 2006. One of the aims of the UKCC was to address concerns of unqualified and inappropriately qualified coaches operating within sports. Other aims were to raise standards of coaching to include agreed national standards of competence amongst coaches at the same level, to tackle a shortage of coaches nationally, and to increase access to high-quality coach education and development. Introduction of the UKCC was a positive step as it necessitated a reflection and analysis of existing, recognized coaching programmes and practice.

Anyone who reaches close to full potential in squash does so with a lot of help, even if that help is an opponent to play with or against. There is a large network of volunteers, including team captains, chair people, treasurers, parents, markers, referees, helpers and not least coaches, to aid in the maintenance and improvement of a player's performance. They come together in the spirit of squash, and often for the betterment of squash.

ES&R, along with Squash Wales, Scottish Squash and Ulster Squash, have formally joined forces to share information and bring together a collective knowledge gained from, and with, the army of volunteers in the squash community. These volunteers make a major contribution in time and effort. High on the list of priorities for squash in the home countries is to harness some of this collective knowledge and formalize it into coach education programmes, in partnership with sports coach UK (scUK), so that all coaches who attend courses and qualify with a UKCC can provide coaching at all levels in a safe, quality assured, professional way that provides the player with pathways to reach full potential and enables them to enjoy a lifetime of squash.

Successful coach education and development programmes change the behaviour and practice of coaches. Here, top coach Mike Harris instructs two of his players.

Who are the Coaches?

Coaches generally are people who have played and, over time, derived great pleasure from squash as a healthy part of their lifestyle.

There are many benefits and ways in which people derive pleasure from squash. These diverse areas of squash activity and enjoyment are often perpetuated by encouraging and guiding others. Parents play a major part in helping, especially with youngsters. Becoming involved with squash can often be an opportunity for quality family time and also provides many opportunities to learn life skills.

Qualities of a Good Coach

Squash was one of the first five sports in the UK to achieve endorsement to deliver UKCC levels 1 to 4, a qualification which is recognized throughout the world. A well-trained, squash UKCC-qualified coach has three essential qualities:

1 **Knowledge** – An in-depth understanding of how squash is played, and won and lost is essential. As explored in depth in Part II of this book, squash is *not* just the ability to strike the ball, but requires the development of a number of *techniques* that come together into rallies. These rallies form the *skill* and allow *tactics* to be developed against an opponent. In other words, we play against an opponent, *not* against the court. The coach's knowledge must embrace all the aspects required by the player. Coaches must develop their own philosophy, which can be likened to electricity; it is not often seen but can carry a punch that can light up the players' lives with a brightness they have not appreciated before.

Also crucial to a coach's knowledge is the ability to recognize the windows of opportunity when young players are ready to learn. Taking advantage of these early learning opportunities increases the success rate dramatically and increases the chances of players reaching full potential. A good coach will never stand still in the search for more knowledge, understanding and its implementation.

2 **Skill of delivery** – The knowledge and understanding must be translated and passed on to the player so that they can perform in a competitive situation; squash is not judged by style or on the practice court. The coach needs also to understand the different ways that people learn and, above all, enable the player to perform the skills practically *in the context of rallies*. A coach must be able to communicate in the following ways:

- *auditory* – through simple, concise description
- *visual* – by demonstration
- *kinaesthetic* – by setting practical exercises.

The *practical application* of the coaches' knowledge to the players that they come into contact with grows into experience and ability.

3 **Personal qualities** – Ideally a coach should take the pledge, be committed and sign up to the Coaches' Code in order to pass on their knowledge in a professional manner. A coach should also enjoy coaching and command respect from others. They must be professional in attitude, which means giving of their best, today and every day. Good coaches will go the extra mile and act as a role model; this influence will develop and set the standard for the players they come into contact with. Coaches should pay attention to how they look and speak well in their deliberations. They should be clear and concise and use simple instructions and demonstrations. They should com-

pliment players sincerely on what they do well and ensure that compliments are *open, honest and above all fair*. They should ask questions, be good listeners and take cognizance of what players say.

The Role of a Coach

Imagine a gardener. Then ask some questions:

- Does the gardener grow the plants or do the plants grow themselves?
- If the gardener plants a rose seed, does a carrot grow?
- Does the gardener provide a lifetime of food and water in one day?
- Does the gardener harvest the plants after only one day?

The analogy is a good one. Here are some answers:

- The coach helps the player but does not make the player
- The coach can only work with the genetic code and get the best from it
- The player will grow and develop at their own pace as the coach drip feeds information
- It will take time for the player to develop.

TOP TIPS FOR COACH/PARENT–PLAYER RELATIONSHIPS

- Discuss squash on the way to squash and while at squash
- Avoid major inquests in the car travelling home
- Only discuss squash at home when the kids raise it
- Provide support rather than indulgence
- Let kids be kids – not mini adults in the land of giants
- Let players learn at their own pace – not the pace that you can coach at
- Coaching, practice and games are the best learning environments
- Enjoy!

The Process of Coaching

Just like the gardener, the coach helps to control the environment in which the player will grow. As with most things, there is a process to coaching and learning.

Firstly, assess the stage of development the player is at. There are a number of ways in which this can be achieved. The most accurate information to measure is:

1   The current playing standard:
    • The player's ability to win games and the level of players that they beat: this shows their ability to compete well
    • Note rankings if available or their position on the club ladder; this shows their ability to perform over a period of time.

2   Assess their tactics
    • How they win or lose points
    • Where on the court do they win or lose points? This is also known as match analysis.

3   Rally building
    • How do they construct rallies?
    • What are they trying to do?
    • Why are they trying to do it?
    • Was it appropriate?
    • How do they execute?

4   Physical ability
    • How much activity is anaerobic?
    • How much activity is aerobic?

5   Psychological
    • focus of attention
    • concentration
    • attitude
    • mindset
    • desire.

6   Lifestyle
    • other interests
    • time available to play.

Secondly, create a record of the findings and a plan of action. Thirdly, deliver a series of sessions that involve:

•   rally building
•   tactics
•   setting some practice routines with clear emphasis
•   setting emphasis for games and matches.

Record the process. Fourthly, re-assess using the same process (Stage 1). Finally, compare the results from the two sets of assessment.

This process will provide a record of improvement for both the player and the coach. The process then repeats itself for the next cycle. The findings will normally show growth, and the same or similar issues may arise as strengths and weaknesses. The findings are relevant to the new level that the player has achieved. The process works like a spiral – you keep arriving at a similar point but in reality the player has moved forward on the journey to reaching their full potential.

Preceding the squash UKCC coaching awards and not on the UK framework is the Leaders Award. This award is aimed at school pupils aged 14–16 and serves as a lead into squash. It is designed to encourage young leaders to assist with squash activities such as marking, officiating, managing, organizing and supervising. There is also a Teachers Award, which is aimed at qualified teachers introducing squash at Key Stages 1 and 2.

An ES&R UKCC-qualified coach, depending on qualification, can undertake the tasks set out in the table below.

TOP TIPS FOR DELIVERING A SESSION

• Set the scene
• Keep them safe
• Evaluate players – what do they need and want?
• Plan sessions – ensure that they progress quickly to game situations
• Provide one piece of information at a time
• Ask questions to check for understanding and learning
• Keep verbal instruction to a minimum; people learn by doing
• Compliment what they do well rather than criticize what they do badly
• Set physical targets and challenges.

LEVELS OF QUALIFICATION OF A SQUASH COACH

Level 4 UKCC	Design, deliver and review long-term specialist plans against specific outcomes
Level 3 UKCC	Design, deliver and review an annual plan
Level 2 UKCC	Design, deliver and review a series of sessions
Level 1 UKCC	Assist a UKCC-qualified coach OR introduce mini squash using teaching cards
Teachers Award	Introduce squash at Key Stages 1 and 2

CHAPTER 6

SUPPORTING PROGRAMMES

Long-Term Athlete Development (LTAD)

Start Them Early

There are many advantages to starting squash at a young age, provided it is grounded in fun; young people learn well during active play. It is important that a range of physical literacy skills are developed early, starting with general skills such as running, throwing, bouncing, catching and striking. School multi-skills programmes often cater for these generic activities, as does *mini-squash,* which is an ES&R skills programme designed to provide an essential and worthy springboard into squash-specific skills, and as the first stage on any player's journey to a lifetime of enjoyment playing squash. Therefore, the links and partnerships between schools and clubs are vital to the overall development of squash players in their formative years.

Many people reading this will have heard about the LTAD model, devised by Istvan Balyi, which has been widely adopted by many sports in the UK. The model has been widely acknowledged amongst sports administrators and policy makers as the 'golden thread' in athlete development, from grassroots to world-class performance. LTAD has helped to stimulate greater thought about talent development and pathways, although the model itself lacks academic validity due to a lack of research providing evidence that it works.

As well as stimulating policy makers to consider talent pathways and development processes, perhaps the main benefit of the LTAD is that it has encouraged organizations to examine player retention strategies and, as a consequence, coaching

processes and a review of how talent can best be developed has ensued. As a result, organizations are arguably better able to plan for the development needs of young players. Therefore, LTAD should be seen as a concept or a philosophy, rather than a programme. This philosophy allows young players and beginners to develop the physical literacy needed to achieve a level of competency in a wide range of skills that exist in all sports. This then allows them to develop a high level of performance for, in our case, squash, where they can grow and achieve their best, and gives them lifelong enjoyment of the game.

The significant aspects incorporated in the LTAD model refer to key periods of training relating to physical maturation, so-called 'windows of adaptation'. These 'windows' indicate when the maximum potential gains in different components of physical fitness can be achieved in young players. For example, strength training should not be introduced too early in a child's physical development. Development needs for players will be unique to each individual but, as a general rule, eight- to twelve-year-olds should develop their aerobic capacity and flexibility, in addition to agility, balance and basic coordination. This is also a good time to further develop the opening of neurological pathways – the process by which information is gathered, processed and acted upon by the brain. This is why, in the early learning stages, it is essential to develop all the skills and attributes required to play a series of squash shots within the context of a rally, and not just feed beginners a set of easy balls to develop their striking technique to the exclusion of other skills. From the age of approximately twelve years, or the onset of puberty, strength and speed training

should be introduced. Speed work can focus upon developing acceleration, agility and reaction speed through short sprints or shuttles.

ES&R Skills Programme

ES&R promotes a three-tiered skills programme for young players, beginning with *mini-squash* and moving onto the *Development Player Awards* and the *TOP Player Awards,* which are specifically designed to incrementally introduce and provide the techniques and skills that allow young players to flourish and enjoy the game in a safe environment. The skills programme also mirrors the Coach Education/Coach Licensing scheme, to ensure that coach education and development, as well as player development, provides the foundations and building blocks that allow coaches and players to enjoy a lifetime involvement.

For more information on mini-squash or the Development Awards please contact one of the UK's national associations.

Competition Structures and Tournaments

Taking part in competitions is one of the best ways to improve. Competition offers all the components, skills and attributes required for success at every level. As highlighted earlier, there are a range of events, festivals and competitions arranged by individual clubs, county associations, national governing bodies and international federations that cater for beginners through to world-class performers: from five-year-olds to the over-seventies. Whatever your ability or age, it is possible to find domestic events in which to participate, whether for social or competitive opportunity. The squash community has traditionally welcomed everyone. For example, within the UK, *mini-squash*, which is designed to introduce an adapted form of squash and develop basic physical literacy for those aged five to eleven years, culminates in squash festivals involving clubs and primary schools. At the opposite end of the age spectrum there is an extensive *masters* programme of events, catering for a number of age groups including those over 35, 40, 45, 50, 55, 60, 65 and 70 years. These events include individual championships, inter-county champion-ships and international representation.

For the more competitive and tal-ented players, there are opportunities to compete for a national ranking and in a national championship at U11. Interna-tional individual and team competition can begin for players in the UK at U13 and this continues through to events for the world's best performers in the form of the World Championships and the World Team Championships. Another accolade of representative squash for players in the UK is the Commonwealth Games, held every four years with both singles and doubles events.

The Women's International Squash Players Association (WISPA) and the Professional Squash Association (PSA) organize the two professional circuits of events for men and women throughout the world where players compete for prize money and world ranking points. These are restricted to members of each respective organization and, of course, a set standard of player/ranking.

The master at work! The touch is all-important.

PART II
TECHNICAL SKILLS

CHAPTER 7

INTRODUCTION AND PHILOSOPHY

Squash is a sport where the situation and/or environment are always changing. When either player strikes the ball, a completely different scenario is created dependent on the trajectory, speed and direction of the ball. The objective is simply to strike the ball so that it strikes the front wall between the *tin* and the *red line* at the top of the court. The ball can strike a side and/or the back wall before striking the front wall. This is done with the intention of forcing one's opponent to make an error. Each player strikes the ball alternately either on the volley or after the ball has bounced once, until either player fails to make a good return.

Many sports are judged quite differently. Sports such as gymnastics, diving, ice skating and synchronized swimming are judged/measured by *style*, where a panel of experienced people mark a performance against an agreed criterion. Athletics, cycling and swimming are judged by *first past the post*. Squash is not judged in either way! As with tennis, badminton, table tennis, boxing and wrestling, squash is judged on the basis of *'one on one direct opposition'*, where two players are matched against each other in direct combat.

What are the Demands on Players?

The demands on squash players to produce good results are many but they can be categorized. In essence, the *true skill* of squash is to engineer/produce a series of *rallies*, which are made up of a vast array of strokes/shots at random. This randomness means that the *prime skills* we need to develop are the ability to:

- **Read** your opponent's actions, which determine where they are going to hit the ball to and what the trajectory is going to be. To then process this information making a
- **Decision** as to what shot you want to play, where you will make contact with it during its flight and to then choose a target. To then produce an
- **Action** or technique of shot that attempts to win the point or at the very least puts your opponent under pressure.

All rallies develop in this sequence, with each player being at a different stage in the sequence at any given time.

The principle of *rallying* stems from the notion of restricting an opponent's options by playing a shot or series of shots that make it difficult for them to hit a winner. A normal start point is to learn to place an opponent under pressure by striking the ball past them into a back corner and trying to create an advantage, opening or loose ball which allows you to attack. Once an advantage is forced/created, many advantages exist to change the rhythm and extend your opponent even further. Should your opponent still make a good return, apply more pressure by changing the rhythm or direction further. The logic is simple. *If you can keep the ball in play then you do have a chance to win the point.*

During the rally it is important to play with as much *accuracy* as possible. The ability to *play the ball from anywhere on the court to anywhere* makes your opponent work hard as they move to the extremities of the court and try to work out what you are doing.

The next objective, in order of importance, would be to *apply as much pressure* on your opponent as possible. This is best done by trying to reduce the *time*

between you striking the ball and your opponent having to strike. The less time you give your opponent, the less time they have to read your actions, process the information, make good decisions and act upon them by moving to the ball on balance to play a good shot.

Closed to Open Skills

Many players deploy most of their effort and focus on the ability to be a shot player, as in just hitting the ball. This is obviously an important aspect of rally building and one of the three key issues of *read–decision–action*, hitting the ball being an action.

A closed skill is easily defined as being a simple action such as striking a ball. An open skill is to read your opponent's actions, making good decisions and acting on them. In other words, *playing the right shot at the right time.* This is best displayed with the *what–why–when–how* principle:

- **What** you are trying to make the ball do, such as target, height, depth, speed, direction etc.
- **Why** you have selected the target and type of shot based on creating the greatest degree of difficulty for your opponent – *tactic!*
- **When** is the appropriate time to play the shot. A great drop shot played to the front of the court would not be effective if your opponent was standing there waiting, but would be a great shot if your opponent was at the back of the court. Be aware that you are playing against an opponent and not the court, so all actions need to be geared towards creating difficulty for your opponent.
- **How** to carry out the prime skills discussed earlier: *read–decision–action.*

CHAPTER 8

TECHNIQUE AND STROKE PRODUCTION

Technique is a simple movement pattern, which in the context of playing squash is the mechanical *'action'* to strike the ball. It is based on the *biomechanical* principles of how the body moves governed by coordination–length of levers–height etc. The *what–why–when–how* principle can be applied to technique.

What you are trying to achieve – Control over the angle, direction and speed of the racket head.

Why you want to control the angle, direction and speed of the racket head – Because the racket head controls the trajectory, speed and accuracy of the ball to the target while achieving the maximum degree of *touch/feel* between the racket head and the ball.

TOP TIPS

- Apply only light pressure with the thumb and forefinger, with the three remaining fingers very loose to provide the maximum degree of *touch/feel* on the ball
- The three remaining fingers need slightly more pressure on the handle for speed and power shots.

When is it appropriate to control the racket head? – Every time that you strike the ball.

How will you achieve control over the racket head? – By gripping the racket handle with the forefinger and thumb in a 'V' shape higher on the handle than the three remaining fingers, so that the handle is cupped gently in the three remaining fingers.

Simple Stroke Production

Backhand and Forehand Driving to Length

What you want to make the ball do – Hit the front wall so that the ball travels as close as possible to the sidewall without clipping, bounces just behind the service box, then fades and dies into the back corner.

Why you want the ball to fade and die into the back corner – A ball which is losing pace or is buried in a back corner increases the degree of difficulty and greatly reduces your opponent's range of options to play a good shot, making it easier for you to read/anticipate their return.

When is it a good time to play a drive to length? – When you're opponent is in a commanding position in the T-zone or they are in a position towards the front of the court.

A good grip that will provide maximum control with high-level touch through the racket.

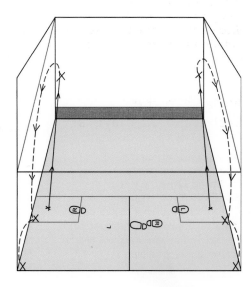

Diagram shows the feet position for a good striking position and the desired path of the ball to a suitable target.

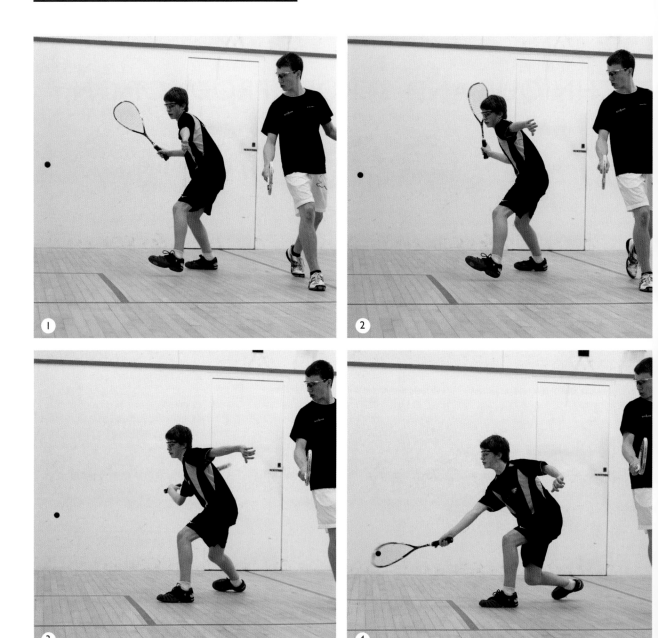

Forehand Drive

Read/watch your opponent closely when they are striking the ball to give an early indication of where they intend to strike the ball. This will give you more time to process the information.

Decide from where during the flight of the ball you will strike. Also decide your target and the type of shot you will play.

Action – Moving from the T-zone, start to raise the racket, moving it up and away from the body. With the last stride on balance, your body weight will be moving

from the right foot towards the left, which is when the upper body begins to turn slightly from right to left and the racket begins its downward and then forward movement to the point of contact. At the point of contact, which is in line with your nose, the racket arm will be at full

Forehand drive to length. All strokes start and finish on or around the T-zone with the last stride on balance for striking and recovery. Numbered in sequence.

extension with the racket head at right angles to the floor. Use the momentum of the racket head to move forward with a throwing action, so that your weight is now on the left foot and able to push and initiate the recovery movement back to the T-zone.

Backhand drive to length. Focus on your opponent's actions to work out which direction you need to move in. Move rhythmically to and from the ball.

Backhand Drive

Read/watch your opponent closely when they are striking the ball to give an early indication of where they intend to strike the ball. This will give you more time to process the information.

Decide early from where you will strike the ball and the target to aim for.

Action – Moving from the T-zone, start to raise the racket, moving up and away from the body. With the last stride on balance, your body weight will be moving from the left foot towards the right, which is when the upper body begins to turn slightly from left to right and the racket begins its downward and then forward movement

to the point of contact. At the point of contact, which is in line with your nose, the racket arm will be at full extension with the racket head at right angles to the floor. Use the momentum of the racket head to move forward so that your weight is now on the right foot and able to push and initiate the recovery movement back to the T-zone.

TOP TIP

- Link your racket action to what the ball does as a result. For example, if you are under-hitting – the ball is landing too short – change the angle of your racket so that the ball strikes higher on the front wall, making it carry further to the back of the court. Be aware of the trajectory and the target the ball reaches, and adjust accordingly. Keep your grip as loose as you can.

SOLO PRACTICE

Start approximately 1.5m from the front wall and gently strike the ball to hit the front wall midway between the tin and the service line. Allow the ball to bounce and repeat. Each time you repeat, move a small step back towards the back wall, adjust the target on the front wall to be slightly higher, and very progressively increase the strength so that the ball bounces on the floor at a comfortable distance from the body to maintain the rally to yourself. When you reach the back wall, progressively move forward one small step at a time, making the same adjustments in reverse. Five minutes on the forehand side and five minutes on the backhand will work wonders!

Backhand and Forehand Sidewall Boasts

What you want to make the ball do – Hit the sidewall then the front wall, bouncing on the floor and fading onto the opposite sidewall.

Why you want the ball to fade onto the sidewall at the front of the court – To force our opponent to move the maximum distance diagonally to the front of the court.

When is it a good time to play a sidewall boast? – When your opponent is behind you at the back of the court or when your opponent is not focused on your actions.

Forehand Boast

Read/watch your opponent closely when they are striking the ball to give an early indication of where they intend to strike the ball. This will give you more time to process the information.

Decide early from where you will strike the ball and the target to aim for.

Action – Moving from the T-zone, start to raise the racket, moving it up and away from the body. With the last stride on

BELOW AND PAGES 36–37: Forehand boast. After moving from the T-zone aim for the sidewall first.

Suitable trajectory and target.

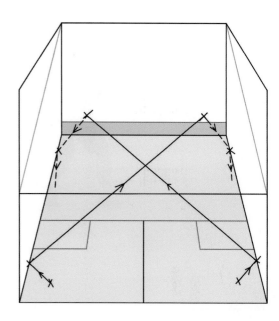

balance, your body weight will be moving from the right foot towards the left, which is when the upper body begins to turn slightly from left to right and the racket begins its downward and then forward movement towards the point of contact. At the point of contact, which is in line with your right ear, the racket arm will be at full extension with the racket head at a slightly open angle and the tip of the racket head just below the level of the playing wrist with a slightly off-centre force coming slightly on the inside of the ball. Use the momentum of the racket head to move forward with a throwing action and a flexible wrist, with a relaxed follow-through to approximately chin height so that your weight is now on the left foot and able to push and assist the recovery movement back to the T-zone.

Backhand Boast

Read/watch your opponent closely when they are striking the ball to give an early indication of where they intend to strike the ball. This will give you more time to process the information.

Decide early from where you will strike the ball and the target to aim for.

Action – Moving from the T-zone, start to raise the racket, moving it up and away from the body. With the last stride on balance, your body weight will be moving from the left foot towards the right, which is when the upper body begins to turn slightly from right to left and the racket begins its downward and then forward movement towards the point of contact. At the point of contact, which is in line with your left ear, the racket arm will be at full extension with the racket head at a slightly open angle and the tip of the racket head just below the level of the playing wrist with a slightly off-centre force coming on the inside of the ball. Use the momentum of the racket head to move forward with a relaxed action and a flexible wrist, with a relaxed follow-through so that your weight is now on the right foot and able to push and assist the recovery movement back to the T-zone.

TOP TIPS

- Watch for your opponent to be caught at the back at the court
- Try to disguise your boast shot to look like a drive to length by subtly changing the angle and direction of your racket head.

ABOVE AND OPPOSITE: *Backhand boast. Aim so the ball will finish near the front corner of the court.*

Drop Shot Straight

What you want to do – Strike the ball with a soft touch and without pace to hit the front wall just above the tin, bouncing on the floor, then fading onto the sidewall.
Why – To draw your opponent up to the front of the court to create distance.
When is it a good time to play a drop shot straight? – When your opponent is off-balance, out of position, or behind the T-zone.

Forehand Drop Shot Straight
Read/watch your opponent closely when they are striking the ball to give an early indication of where they intend to strike the ball. This will give you more time to process the information.
Decide from where you will strike the ball, preferably early and when the ball is at its highest point or just before, and the target to aim for.
Action – Moving from the T-zone, start to raise the racket, moving it up and away from the body. On the last stride your body weight will be moving from the right foot towards the left, which is when the upper body begins to turn slightly from right to left and the racket begins its downward and then forward movement towards

Desired trajectory and target.

the point of contact. At the point of contact, which is in line with your left ear, the racket arm will be at full extension with the racket head at a slightly open angle and the tip of the racket head just below the level of the playing wrist with a slightly off-centre force, in other words a little side

spin and soft touch coming on the inside of the ball. Use the momentum of the racket head to move forward with a slow, gentle follow-through to approximately chest height, so that your weight is now on the left foot and able to push and assist the recovery movement back to the T-zone.

Forehand drop shot straight. Try to keep the whole body relaxed while moving to and from the ball.

Backhand Drop Shot Straight

Read/watch your opponent closely when they are striking the ball to give an early indication of where they intend to strike the ball. This will give you more time to process the information.

Decide early from where you will strike the ball and the target to aim for.

Action – Moving from the T-zone, start to raise the racket, moving it up and away from the body. On the last stride your body weight will be moving from the left foot towards the right, which is when

the upper body begins to turn slightly from left to right and the racket begins its downward and then forward movement towards the point of contact. At the point of contact, which is in line with your right

ear, the racket arm will be at full extension with the racket head at a slightly open angle and the tip of the racket head just below the level of the playing wrist with a slightly off-centre force, in other words a little side spin and soft touch coming on the inside of the ball. Use the momentum of the racket head to move forward with a slow, gentle follow-through to approximately chest height, so that your weight is now on the right foot and able to push and assist the recovery movement back to the T-zone.

Backhand drop shot straight. After moving into position try to keep your grip relaxed.

Drop Shots Cross-Court

What you want to do – Strike the ball with a soft touch and without pace to hit the front wall just above the tin, bouncing on the floor, then fading onto the sidewall or nick between wall and floor.

Why – To draw your opponent up to the front of the court to create distance.

When is it a good time to play a drop shot cross-court? – When your opponent is off-balance, out of position or behind the T-zone.

Forehand Drop Shot Cross-Court

Read/watch your opponent closely when they are striking the ball to give an early indication of where they intend to strike the ball. This will give you more time to process the information.

Decide from where you will strike the ball, preferably early and when the ball is at its highest point or just before, and the target to aim for.

Action – Moving from the T-zone, start to raise the racket, moving it up and away from the body. On the last stride, your

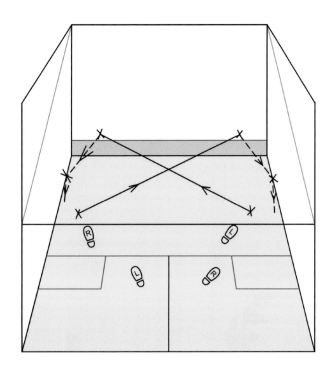

Desired trajectory and target.

As this image demonstrates, good stroke preparation is important for any form of drop shot.

body weight will be moving from the right foot towards the left, which is when the upper body begins to turn slightly from right to left and the racket begins its downward and then forward movement towards the point of contact. At the point of contact, which is in line with the left foot, the racket arm will be at full extension and the racket head at a slightly open angle using a soft touch with the point of contact on the outside of the ball. Use the momentum of the racket head to move sideways with a slow, gentle follow-through to approximately chest height so that your weight is now on the left foot and able to push and assist the recovery movement back to the T-zone.

Backhand Drop Shot Cross-Court

Read/watch your opponent closely when they are striking the ball to give an early indication of where they intend to strike the ball. This will give you more time to process the information.

Decide early from where you will strike the ball and the target to aim for.

Action – Moving from the T-zone, start to raise the racket, moving it up and away from the body. On the last stride, your body weight will be moving from the left foot towards the right, which is when the upper body begins to turn slightly from left to right and the racket begins its downward and then forward movement towards the point of contact. At the point of contact, which is in line with the right foot, the racket arm will be at full extension with the racket head at a slightly open angle using a soft touch with the point of contact on the outside of the ball. Use the momentum of the racket head to move sideways with a slow, gentle follow-through to approximately chest height so that your weight is now on the right foot and able to push and assist the recovery movement back to the T-zone.

TOP TIP

- Grip the racket with a slight tension of the thumb and forefinger, relaxing the three remaining fingers.

In this photograph, the player is clearly well balanced and ready to strike the ball.

Cross-Court Drive to Length Backhand and Forehand

What you want to do – Hit the front wall just off centre so that the ball will travel to a point on the sidewall just behind the service box, fading at the back of the court.

Why – To force your opponent as far from the T-zone as possible, allowing you to command the T-zone.

When is it a good time to play a cross-court drive? – When your opponent is at the front of the court or on the other side of the court.

Forehand Cross-Court Drive to Length

Read/watch your opponent closely when they are striking the ball to give an early indication of where they intend to strike the ball. This will give you more time to process the information.

Decide early from where you will strike the ball and the target to aim for.

Action – The forehand cross-court drive is often played off the so-called *wrong foot* – with the right foot nearest the sidewall – usually from a single step and striking the ball while moving back to the T-zone. At this point your body weight will be moving from the right foot to the left, which is also when the upper body is turning from facing the sidewall slightly from right to left and the racket begins its downward and then forward movement to the point of contact. At the point of contact, which is in line with your non-playing shoulder, the racket arm will be at full extension at the point of contact, with the racket head at right angles to the floor or slightly open and just on the outer side of the ball. Use the momentum of the racket head to continue moving forward with a slapping action, so that the follow-through finishes at approximately chest height, having come across the upper body with your weight on the left foot and back on the T-zone.

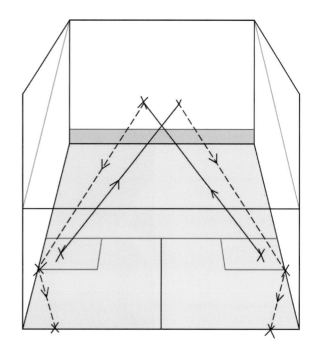

Desired trajectory and target.

Forehand cross-court to length. Be prepared to strike it with good pace.

Backhand Cross-Court Drive to Length

Read/watch your opponent closely when they are striking the ball to give an early indication of where they intend to strike the ball. This will give you more time to process the information.

Decide early from where you will strike the ball and the target to aim for.

Action – Moving from the T-zone, start to raise the racket, moving it up and away from the body. On the last stride, your body weight will be moving from the left foot towards the right, which is when the upper body begins to turn slightly from left to right and the racket begins its downward and then forward movement to the point of contact. At the point of contact, which is in front of your playing shoulder, the racket arm will be at full extension with the racket head at right angles to the floor or slightly open. Use the momentum of the racket head to move forward so that the follow-through finishes at approximately chest height, having come slightly across the upper body, with your weight on the right foot and able to push and enable the recovery movement back to the T-zone.

TOP TIPS

- Try to hit the ball with good pace
- Grip the racket with the main tension in the middle finger, forefinger and thumb.

Backhand cross-court to length. Focus on good accuracy away from your opponent.

Straight and Cross-Court Lob to Length

What you want the ball to do – To drop as near vertical as possible in a back corner. Strike the ball to hit high on the front wall and arc as high as possible with slow to medium pace.

Why play a high lob? – To 'buy' time to recover back to the T-zone and reduce your opponent's options and variation of pace.

When is it a good time to play a lob? – When your opponent is in a commanding position on the T-zone or at the front of the court.

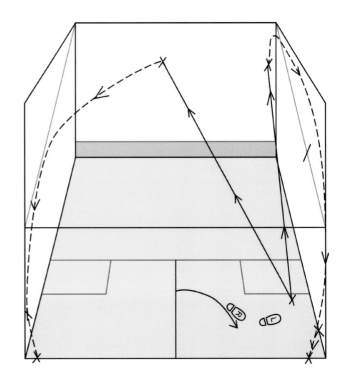

RIGHT: *Desired trajectory and target.*

LEFT AND ABOVE: Backhand cross-court lob. Try to keep the body stable on contact.

Forehand Cross-Court Lob

Read/watch your opponent closely when they are striking the ball to give an early indication of where they intend to strike the ball. This will give you more time to process the information.

Decide early from where you will strike the ball and the target to aim for.

Action – Moving from the T-zone start to raise the racket, moving it up and away from the body. On the last stride your body weight will be moving towards the sidewall, which is when the upper body begins to turn slightly to face the sidewall and the racket begins its downward and then forward movement to the point of contact. At the point of contact, which is in front of your leading foot, and with the playing arm at full extension with the racket head parallel to the floor, use the momentum of the racket head to move forwards and upwards, making contact with the bottom part of the ball with a lifting action and the follow-through travel-

ling in an upward arc. The leading foot pushes to assist the movement back to the T-zone.

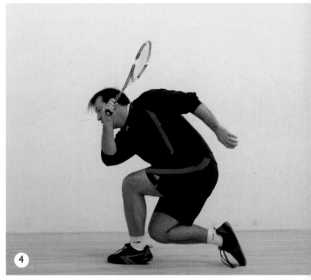

LEFT AND ABOVE: Forehand cross-court lob. Relaxed follow-through and recovery.

CHAPTER 9

DEVELOPING A SKILFUL GAME

In the context of playing squash, 'skill' is the coming together of all the components that make up a good performance in a game situation. Skill is the proficiency in a match situation that comes from awareness and understanding of how squash is played, competed for, won and lost through training, practice and experience in the match environment. Skill in its most basic form is the practical application of the principles discussed earlier, in the sequence *read–decision–action*.

All rallies are bult this way.

The best learning environments for the continuous development of skill are listed below.

Coaching or learning through observation. Watching good players, observing what they do and how they do it, backed up in open debate with coaches and other players, will enhance the developmental process and learning.

Practice. It is important to practise progressively and to simulate a realistic game situation. Knowledge and understanding without the application of what to do is only the starting point. Practice will refine your skills over time.

Competition. The techniques, skills and attributes are put to the test in competition, which is why competition is arguably the best learning environment for a budding squash player.

Movement

In the context of squash, movement is a change in position to bring about the desired result, which is that the ball reaches the selected target. Movement plays a major role in bringing together all the components of rally building. It acts as the cement that binds the building blocks of the rally together.

> **TOP TIPS**
>
> - Try to play games with players better than you in order to learn new things
> - Try to play at your own standard to develop good tactics
> - Play a level down from your current standard to learn how to hit point-winning shots.

Last stride on balance. Keep your body as stable as possible.

If squash were only about the ability to strike the ball, then movement would be almost redundant. As mentioned previously, squash requires that we read our opponent's actions, make decisions on what we want to do and then act upon what we have read and chosen to do. In other words, you may be able to strike the ball but if you are unable to get to the ball then the rally will end.

A fair description of movement in squash is that we 'move to a position where we have chosen to strike the ball from,' then with the last stride on balance we can strike the ball and recover back to the T-zone, which is the most central position on the court to enable us to cover all further options. *Balance* plays an important part in the process of movement. Three principles must be applied for balance to be maintained.

Feet position. The feet should always be wider than the shoulders for good stability, though maybe not this wide if possible!

1   The *area of base* of the body, which in practical terms is the position of the feet. If the feet are close together the area of base is narrow, hence balance will be impeded. If the feet are wider apart the base is wider, hence balance will be increased but will inhibit recovery.

2   The *height of the centre of gravity* (C of G) of the body is the central point where the body is weighted, balanced or centred. If the player adopts a crouched stance the C of G will be lowered. If the player raises his arms then the C of G will be raised.

3   The *horizontal distance between the C of G and either foot.* If the player leans in either direction, the horizontal distance will be lengthened in one direction and shortened in the opposite direction. Hence the degree of balance will be increased in the direction the distance is increased and decreased in the direction the distance is decreased

Science backs up what players and coaches have been saying for years; there are many different movements in squash. When we move, we use all the joints of the body – *summation of joint forces* – with the force starting in the feet, pushing against the

At the limit. Get down low to get the maximum reach.

Not too much of a stretch. Stretch too far and it is difficult to recover.

Total focus and ready to go. That first step must be quick.

TOP TIPS FOR MOVEMENT

- Be focused on your opponent's racket action immediately prior to them striking so you can *read* their actions
- Be poised ready to move quickly, pushing off quickly
- Begin racket preparation in these early steps
- Make the last stride on balance, using the trailing foot as a brake
- Keep your shoulders behind your leading foot for maximum stability
- Recover quickly back to the T-zone.

ground and working through the whole body in sequence. The initial movement from the T-zone – *continuance of joint forces* – starts with a series of small compensatory movements, known in squash as a *split step*. This occurs while the player is reading/anticipating where the opponent is going to hit the ball, which determines the direction in which they will have to move.

The foot farthest from the direction in which the player moves will produce the force against the floor to set the body in motion to arrive at the position chosen to strike the ball from, with the last stride on balance to enable a stable base from which to strike the ball. At this point the leading foot then pushes against the floor to start the recovery movement back to the T-zone, using the momentum of the follow-through to assist the process. If the joints of the body are not used in the right sequence, the movement will be slow, un-coordinated, and lack rhythm, stability and speed.

Many movements in squash are unpredictable, multi-directional, variable in speed and occur in any combination. They include:

* split step
* running
* side steps
* lunging
* jumping and
* squatting.

Also essential to this movement process is *core stability*, a term used to describe the strength and stability in the middle of the body (stomach and back muscles) that links moving and striking in squash. It is common to see players without good core stability move to a good position only to be unstable when striking, which severely inhibits accuracy and creates major problems recovering back to the T-zone.

Rally Building

Philosophy

Have you ever watched the truly great players and thought to yourself that they have so much time, never have to move, and are just standing there ready to play the ball? They always make good decisions as to where to put the ball, when to put it there and execute shots with great accuracy and deception.

Not long ago I was talking with a world-class player and asked the question: 'What do you feel are the largest contributing factors that make you arguably the best player in the world?' The answer was 'My speed.' To which I asked:

* Is it the speed at which you read what your opponent is doing?
* Is it the speed at which you process all that information?
* Is it the speed at which you make your decisions as to what you are going to play and where to play it?
* Is it the speed at which you are able to move to where you have chosen to strike the ball from?
* Is it the speed at which you are capable of striking the ball?
* Is it the speed at which you can recover back to the T-zone?

The answer came back quickly: 'All of them!'

This true story supports what we already know – that the great players have learned not just what to do but *how* to do

it. It also reflects the research of sports scientists, which indicates that these skills are learned through the following pathways.

* **Learning from other players or coaches.** By studying how good players build rallies to put their opponents under pressure and win points.
* **Deliberate practice** with specific aims, expectations and focus. Practice is monitored through observation of what can be improved upon through repetition and successive refinement. To gain maximum benefit from any feedback, players need to practise their rally building with full concentration and effort. Players must stretch themselves to gain benefit during

On the ball early with lots of options. If you are quick you can do whatever you like.

Delay for good disguise. Just hold for a split second to keep your opponent guessing.

deliberate practice. These improvements can be transferred across and reflected in competition.

- **Competition.** This is where the skills and attributes come together in a series of rallies that make up games and matches.

In order to build a rally many things need to come together, so we need to consider the following questions.

What are we trying to achieve and what do we want to make the ball do, *target – trajectory – speed* etc? At this level of development we need to ensure that everything comes together at the same time, in other words we need to bring all the elements together to work in unison. In addition to maintaining the rally through the *read – decision – action* system, a player must have the ability to play the ball from anywhere in the court to anywhere with great accuracy and variation/deception. Remember that we are trying to win the point or, at the very least, put our opponent under as much constant *pressure* as possible.

Why choose a particular *tactic* to achieve the best possible advantage? The answer to this question is based on:

When it would be most appropriate to try to achieve this *tactic*. The best time is when your opponent is out of position. For example, if your opponent is at the front of the court then play the ball to the back.

How you put together the sequence of events that will bring about this *outcome* using the method of *read – anticipate – read*. This is done by focusing your attention carefully on your opponent's body language, specifically their racket action prior to them making contact with the ball. It is this part of their action that will determine the trajectory and speed of the ball, thus providing you with maximum information, visual cues, and time to predict and track the path of the ball.

The **speed** with which you process this information. Speed assists greatly in making an early *decision* of target and shot selection while moving into a striking zone and starting the racket preparation to arrive with the last stride on balance.

Action/technique of striking the ball using the follow-through to assist the recovery movement back to the T-zone ready for the whole process to start again.

Progressive Rally Building

The overall objective of rally building is for the player to learn to play squash in the *game situation*. As discussed earlier, no player is awarded points for looking technically good; the prime aim in rally building is to bring all the major skills and attributes together, judged by the effectiveness to apply pressure to an opponent to win points and ultimately matches.

TOP TIPS FOR RALLY BUILDING

- Try to learn new things and practise in the context of a rally/match
- The rule: if it happens in a match, practise it – if it doesn't happen in a match, don't.

Essential to this process is to practise close to the limit of your current level of play and development. The quality of learning and practice is important, *not* just the amount. Many people will have heard the saying *'perfect practice makes perfect'*. In squash terms the word perfect also

Progressive rally building

means in the context of the rally/game/match.

In the first phase of rally building, it helps if the routine is done with a high level of co-operation. This is essentially to establish a rhythm of movement while learning to *isolate the visual cues of body language* and *the racket action just before contact.*

As the routine progresses through stages, different shots are introduced until all areas of the court are being targeted. The routine then progresses further with an additional range of shots. These will increase the pace and decrease your opponent's organizational time by taking the ball early, for example volleying.

The diagram opposite shows the different phases of rally building. Start with two players both playing to a length, circling around each other back to the T-zone after each shot, with both players looking to drive the ball to force the opponent into the back corner and take command of the T-zone (*one corner*). When either player takes command of the T-zone in front of their opponent, they play an attacking boast. The opponent moves to the front on the opposite side of the court and plays a cross-court drive to length and the rally continues to a length (*two corners*). After the boast, the receiver has the option of playing the ball cross-court to length *or* straight to length. The rally continues to length on the same wall (*three corners*). After the boast, the receiver has the option of straight, cross-court to length *or* a cross-court drop. The rally continues on the current wall to length (*four corners*). Increase the range of shots progressively from each quarter, for example drop the boast/lob the drop/boast the boast etc.

The greater the variation/randomness you can produce, the greater the opportunity to:

- force your opponent to guess rather than read/anticipate your actions
- add to the time that your opponent has to take to work out your tactics
- buy you additional time.

Build and Backtrack Rallies

This is another way to build on and move from technique into skill. It is a way of progressing from closed to open skills, and teaches the player to learn (*read*) how to isolate the visual signals of their opponent's racket actions to determine where they are going to hit the ball.

- Player A decides on a good service and practises the same service for 2min
- Player B, in response, decides on the strongest possible receive, which is practised for the same 2min with player A catching the ball to serve again
- Changeover – player B decides on a service etc. – 2min
- Player A uses same service – player B the same receive – player A decides on the best possible third ball – player B decides on the best fourth ball etc. – 2min
- Changeover – 2min
- Player A uses same first ball – player B uses same second ball – player A uses same third ball – player B uses same fourth ball – player A decides on the strongest possible fifth ball – player B the strongest possible sixth ball – 2min
- Changeover – 2min

The process then changes from playing to a specific pattern to one that becomes progressively random.

- Player B going to a random target on the sixth ball and both players going to random targets to the completion of the rally – 2min
- Changeover – 2min
- Player B going to a random target on the fifth ball and both players going to random targets to the completion of the rally – 2min
- Changeover – 2min

- Player B going to a random target on the fourth ball – play the rally out – 2min
- Changeover – 2min
- Player B going to a random target on the second ball – play the rally out – 2min
- Changeover – 2min

More Advanced Strokes

In the context of squash, disguise is the 'ability to conceal what you are trying to do' by making your body language and racket action look the same for each shot that you play. Disguise plays a major role in advanced stroke play and rally building. For example, the action of striking the ball to length is different from when playing a side-wall boast. This is accomplished by changing the racket angle and direction. Making the early racket preparation to the ball the same for each shot and delaying the subtle changes of angle and direction to the last microsecond will have the effect of reducing your opponent's reading and decision-making time, so inhibiting their ability to play on balance and with acute accuracy. This gives you more time, which ultimately means less effort, more accuracy and the opportunity to apply more *pressure*!

Benefits of Volley

To strike the ball on the volley you need the ability not only to hit the ball before it has bounced but also to take the ball much earlier. A common piece of advice from coaches and good players is 'Take the ball early, early and early.' If in any doubt, take the ball earlier, even if it means that you are a little off-balance when making contact. Remember that part of the nature of competition is to put your opponent under so much pressure that they are off-balance when playing the ball. This will be easier to do when you are moving forward as opposed to backwards. See pages 58–60 for some good examples of volleying.

A - Red

B - Green

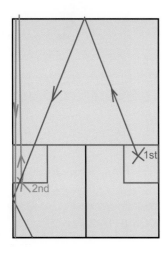

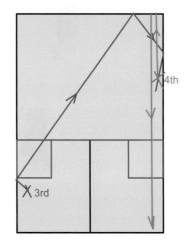

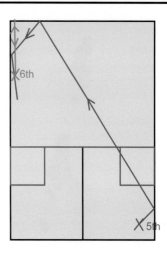

ABOVE: Chosen targets for A and B.

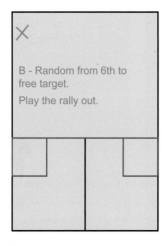

B - Random from 6th to free target.

Play the rally out.

A - Random from 6th to free target.

Play the rally out.

B - Random from 4th to free target.

Play the rally out.

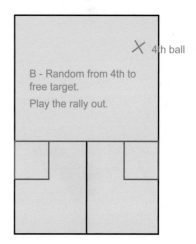

ABOVE AND RIGHT: Working back from specific targets to a totally random rally.

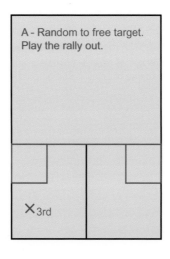

A - Random to free target. Play the rally out.

B - Random to free target. Play the rally out.

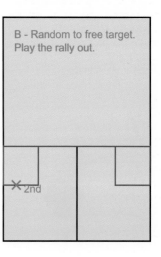

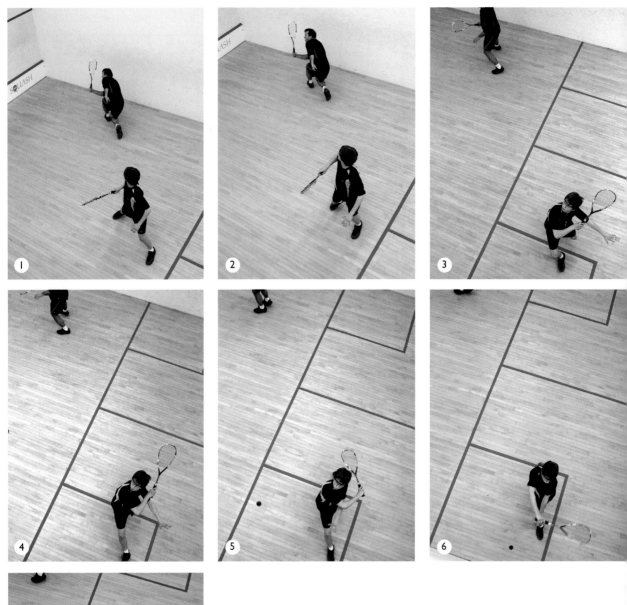

THIS PAGE: Good examples of volleying. Take the ball as early as possible, even at the expense of being a little off balance.

RIGHT: Example of a good volley. From the T-zone focus on your opponent's racket action. Track the ball and force yourself to meet the ball very early. Strike with as much accuracy as possible with medium tension in your grip.

Look for every opportunity when you have forced your opponent into giving you a semi loose ball. Go with your first instinct to volley. Keeping your body agile without much tension, strike the ball away from your opponent.

Straight Volleys to Length

What you want to do – Strike the ball as early as is possible before it bounces. This often means that you will have to strike off the so-called *wrong foot* and possibly be a little off-balance. Aim to hit the front wall so that the ball will travel and bounce just behind the service box, then fade and die into the back of the court.

Why – To severely reduce your opponent's organization and decision-making time in order to force the error. We want the ball to fade and die into the back of the court in the shortest possible time from you striking it. A ball that is losing pace in a back corner increases the degree of difficulty and greatly reduces the range of options of your opponent to play a good shot, making it easier for you to anticipate/read their return.

When is it a good time to play a straight volley drive to length – When your opponent is in a commanding position in the T-zone or in a position towards the front of the court.

Forehand Volley to Length

Read/watch your opponent closely when they are striking the ball to give an early indication of where they intend to strike the ball. This will give you more time to process the information.

Decide early that you will strike the ball as early as possible and before it bounces, and decide the target to aim for.

Action – Moving from the T-zone start to raise the racket, moving it up and away from the body. On the last stride your body weight will be moving from the back foot to the front foot, which is when the upper body begins to turn slightly to face the sidewall and the racket begins its slightly downward and forward movement to the point of contact. At the point of contact, which is in front of your front foot, and with the racket head at full extension and at right angles to the floor, use the momentum of the racket head to move forward with a throwing action so that your weight is now definitely on the front foot and able to push and enable the recovery movement back to the T-zone.

Backhand Volley to Length

Read/watch your opponent closely when they are striking the ball to give an early indication of where they intend to strike the ball. This will give you more time to process the information.

Decide early that you will strike the ball as early as possible and before it bounces, and decide the target to aim for.

Action – Moving from the T-zone start to raise the racket, moving it up and away from the body. On the last stride your body weight will be moving from

Take the advantage when you can. If you don't, your opponent will.

When all the good points are there – then magic is in the air.

On perfect balance.

the back foot to the front foot, which is when the upper body begins to turn slightly to face the sidewall and the racket begins its slightly downward and forward movement to the point of contact. At the point of contact, which is in front of your front foot, and with the racket head at full extension and at right angles to the floor, use the momentum of the racket head to move forward with a throwing action so that your weight is now definitely on the front foot and able to push and enable the recovery movement back to the T-zone.

Volley Boasts

What you want to do – Strike the ball as early as is possible before it bounces.

This often means that you will have to strike off the so-called *wrong foot* and possibly be a little off-balance. Aim to hit the sidewall so that the ball will travel to the front wall, bounce and die on the sidewall as near to the front and sidewalls as possible.

Why – To severely reduce your opponent's organization and decision-making time in order to force the error. We want the ball to fade and die on the sidewall in the shortest possible time from you striking it and your opponent having to strike it. A ball that is losing pace near to a sidewall increases the degree of difficulty and greatly reduces the range of options of your opponent to play a good shot, making it easier for you to read their return.

When is it a good time to play a volley boast? – When your opponent is caught behind you, still trying to recover from their previous shot.

Forehand Volley Boast

Read/watch and focus on your opponent's actions closely when they are striking the ball to give an early indication of where they intend to strike the ball. This will give you more time to process the information.

Decide early that you will strike the ball as early as possible and on the volley.

Action – Moving from the T-zone start to raise the racket, moving it up and away from the body. On the last stride your body weight will be moving from the back foot to the front foot, which is when

The master, Nick Matthew, at work. A classic shot with the balance just perfect..

Lining up for a good forehand volley boast. A clear focus is essential.

the upper body begins to turn slightly to face the sidewall and the racket begins its downward and forward movement to the point of contact. At the point of contact, which is in front of your back foot, and with the racket head at full extension and slightly open, use the momentum of the racket head to move forward with a throwing action, so that your weight is now definitely on the front foot and able to push and enable the recovery movement back to the T-zone.

Backhand Volley Boast

Read/watch your opponent closely when they are striking the ball to give an early indication of where they intend to strike the ball. This will give you more time to process the information.

Decide early that you will strike the ball as early as possible and before it bounces, and decide the target to aim for.

Action – Moving from the T-zone start to raise the racket, moving it up and away from the body. On the last stride your body weight will be moving from the back foot to the front foot, which is when the upper body begins to turn slightly to face the sidewall and the racket begins its downward and forward movement to the point of contact. At the point of contact, which is in front of your back foot, and with the racket head at full extension and slightly open, use the momentum of the racket head to move forward with a throwing action, so that your weight is now definitely on the front foot and able to push and enable

the recovery movement back to the T-zone.

Volley Drops

What you want to do – Strike the ball as early as possible before it bounces with a soft to medium touch and without pace to hit the front wall just above the tin, bouncing on the floor then fading onto the sidewall.

Why – To draw your opponent up to the front of the court.

When is it a good time to play a volley drop? – When your opponent is off-balance, out of position or behind the T-zone.

Take the advantage when you can. Go with your instinct. A well executed drop shot is often a point winner.

Forehand Volley Drop Shot Straight

Read/watch your opponent closely when they are striking the ball to give an early indication of where they intend to strike the ball. This will give you more time to process the information.

Decide early from where you will strike the ball, preferably as early as possible, and on the volley at a high point during its trajectory.

Action – Moving from the T-zone start to raise the racket, moving it up and away from the body. On the last stride your body weight will be moving from the back foot to the front foot, which is when the upper body begins to turn slightly to face a sidewall and the racket begins its downward and then forward movement towards the point of contact. At the point of contact, which is in line with your front foot or before, the racket arm will be at full extension with the racket head at a slightly open angle and with a soft to medium touch coming forwards and down on the ball so imparting a slight backspin. Use the momentum of the racket head to move forward with a slow, gentle follow-through to approximately chest height, so that your weight is now on the front foot and able to push and assist the recovery movement back to the T-zone.

Backhand Volley Drop Shot Straight

Read/watch your opponent closely when they are striking the ball to give an early indication of where they intend to strike the ball. This will give you more time to process the information.

Decide early from where you will strike the ball, preferably as early as possible and on the volley at a high point during its trajectory.

Action – Moving from the T-zone start to raise the racket, moving it up and away from the body. On the last stride your body weight will be moving from the back foot to the front foot, which is when the upper body begins to turn slightly to face a sidewall and the racket begins its downward and then forward movement towards the point of contact. At the point of contact, which is in line with your front foot or before, the racket arm will be at full extension with the racket head at a slightly open angle, and with a soft to

Eye on the ball with good concentration.

Keep the pressure on. If you don't – your opponent will.

medium touch coming forwards and down on the ball so imparting a slight backspin. Use the momentum of the racket head to move forward with a slow, gentle follow-through to approximately chest height, so that your weight is now on the front foot and able to push and assist the recovery movement back to the T-zone.

Volley Angle Kills

What you want to do – Strike the ball with considerable pace, hitting the front wall just above the tin and then the nick between the sidewall and the floor so that the ball rolls rather than bounces off the floor.

Why – To finish the rally with the ball dead on the court before your opponent has time to react.

When is it a good time to play a volley angle kill? – When you have forced your opponent to play a loose shot, so the ball is away from the sidewall and high in the court.

Backhand Volley Angle Kill

Read/watch for when you have your opponent under pressure or unbalanced. This is when you are more likely to get a loose high ball.

Decide early from where you will strike the ball and the target to aim for.

Action – As you move forward and raise the racket head with the last stride on balance, your body weight will be moving forward and the upper body turning slightly to the left. With the racket head above the ball, swing forwards and down-wards, making contact on the outside of the ball at approximately 11 o'clock ahead of your leading foot, imparting some side spin with medium to firm touch. Continue

A leap of faith. Sometimes you just have to take a chance.

to follow-through with your weight start-ing to push back from the leading foot towards the T-zone.

Forehand Volley Angle Kill

Read/watch for when you have your opponent under pressure or unbalanced. This is when you are more likely to get a loose high ball.

Decide early from where you will strike the ball and the target to aim for.

Action – As you move forward and raise the racket head with the last stride on balance, your body weight will be moving forward and the upper body turning slightly to the right. With the racket head above the ball, swinging forwards and downwards, make contact on the outside

of the ball at approximately 2 o'clock ahead of your leading foot, imparting some side spin with medium to firm touch. Continue to follow-through with your weight, starting to push back from the leading foot towards the T-zone.

Straight Volley Kill

What you want to do – Strike the ball with as much force as you can in order to hit the front wall just above the tin, then the side-wall, bouncing as soon as possible so that the ball is rolling before the service box.

Why – To finish the rally with the ball dead on the court before your opponent has time to react.

When is it a good time to play a straight volley kill? – When you have forced your opponent to play a loose shot, with the ball just off the sidewall and high in the court.

Backhand Straight Volley Kill

Read/watch for when you have your opponent under pressure or unbalanced. This is when you are more likely to get a loose high ball.

Decide early from where you will strike the ball and the target to aim for.

Action – As you move forward and raise the racket head with the last stride on balance, your body weight will be moving forward and the upper body turning slightly to the left. With the racket head

It is possible from here. Be brave and the reward of a point can be yours.

Worth a try. Follow your first instinct and be as quick as possible to apply maximum pressure on your opponent.

Decide early from where you will strike the ball and the target to aim for.
Action – As you move forward and raise the racket head with the last stride on balance, your body weight will be moving forward and the upper body turning slightly to the right. With the racket head above the ball, swinging forwards and downwards, make contact level with your front foot on the back of the ball, imparting backspin.

Cross-Court Volley Drop

What you want to do – Strike the ball without pace to hit the front wall just above the tin and then the nick between the sidewall and floor so that the ball rolls rather than bounces off the floor.
Why – To finish the rally with the ball dead on the court before your opponent has time to react.
When is it a good time to play a cross-court volley drop? – When you have forced your opponent to play a loose shot, with the ball away from the sidewall and high in the court.

Backhand Cross-Court Volley Drop
Read/watch for when you have your opponent under pressure or unbalanced. This is when you are more likely to get a loose high ball.
Decide early from where you will strike the ball and the target to aim for.
Action – As you move forward and raise the racket head with the last stride on balance, your body weight will be moving forward and the upper body turning slightly to the left. With the racket head above the ball, swinging forwards and downwards, make contact on the outside of the ball at approximately 11 o'clock ahead of your leading foot, imparting some side spin with medium to light touch.

above the ball, swinging forwards and downwards, make contact level with your front foot on the back of the ball, imparting backspin.

Forehand Straight Volley Kill
Read/watch for when you have your opponent under pressure or unbalanced. This is when you are more likely to get a loose high ball.

In a situation like the one depicted here, the player has to decide whether to opt for a safety shot or try for a winner.

Continue to follow-through with your weight starting to push back from the leading foot towards the T-zone.

Forehand Cross-Court Volley Drop

Read/watch for when you have your opponent under pressure or they are unbalanced. This is when you are more likely to get a loose high ball.

Decide early from where you will strike the ball and the target to aim for.

Action – As you move forward and raise the racket head with the last stride on balance, your body weight will be moving forward and the upper body turning slightly to the right. With the racket head above the ball, swinging forwards and downwards, make contact on the outside of the ball at approximately 2 o'clock ahead of your leading foot, imparting some side spin with medium to light touch. Continue to follow-through with your weight starting to push back from the leading foot towards the T-zone.

Trickle Boasts Backhand and Forehand

What you want the ball to do – Without pace to strike the sidewall and then the front wall marginally above the tin, dying on the floor as near to the front wall as possible.

Why – To deceive your opponent as to your selected target to win the rally outright and/or to draw your opponent out of position and place them under pressure.

When is it a good time to play the shot? – When your opponent is away from the T-zone, off-balance and/or when they are not looking.

How

Read/watch for when your opponent is not fully focused on your action.

From a position like this, it is easy to hit a winner if the player remains calm and collected.

Decide – Leave your decision as late as possible to decrease your opponent's reading time.

Action – On the forward part of your swing, drop your racket head sharply to strike the inside of the ball at approximately 4 o'clock for backhand (8 o'clock for forehand), applying some side spin.

TOP TIP

- With a very relaxed grip and with a medium-paced swing, strike the ball with an off-centre force so that the ball comes off the racket head slower than with an on-centre force, adding to the deception.

CHAPTER 10

TACTICS AND MAKING IT ALL WORK

In the context of squash, tactics can be described as 'a plan or set of practical actions to promote a desired result.' Contrary to some people's view, squash operates to patterns of play. In its most obvious sense, players attack, defend, counter-attack, play with pace, without pace. We all have strengths and weaknesses and players will use their strengths while playing to an opponent's weaknesses. The variation that players can produce when adopting tactics is crucial to all players' degree of success. The greater the degree of variation, the greater the effect of overloading information that your opponent must *read* and *process*, resulting in loose play and creating more opportunities for you to play winning shots.

The key is to have a plan or series of tactical ploys that you have prepared for your practice and training, preferably based on analysis of your likely opponents.

High on the list of priorities for tactics to be effective is a *command of the T-zone.*

The T-zone is the most central position on the court, being the most equal distance to any area that you may be forced to move to. It is very important that you spend as little time away from the T-zone as possible, and that any movement away from this area be compensated with an immediate and hasty return.

The practical application required to achieve a desired tactical result will include the **DOT** principle.

Some times desperate measures are called for.

D (distance). Try to make your opponent move the greatest distance to get to the ball. The further your opponent moves, the more time it takes, the quicker he will become tired and the more likely he will not be on balance to play a good shot, which increases your opportunity to play a winner.

O (opportunity). The more pressure you can apply, the more opportunities you create to hit winners. Playing with great accuracy and variation has a profound effect on your opponent's options and ability to play good shots; the result being that it is easier for you to read your opponent's actions and make an early decision.

T (time). Try to take the ball as early as possible. This will reduce the time from you striking the ball to when your opponent has to strike. The less time available to your opponent severely reduces their movement, decision-making and organization time, often forcing an error or forcing them to take the ball much later. If they take the ball 0.5sec later, it also takes 0.5sec for the ball to get level to where they could have taken it. Hence, if they gain the 0.5sec by taking the ball late, then you gain an extra 1.0sec, giving you even more opportunity.

Standard Tactics

Standard tactics is a series of *patterns of play* designed to apply pressure on a player's opponent. A series of rallies can be built and used at random. For example

- using four different standard rallies used totally at random and changing constantly provides twenty-four different variations to keep your opponent guessing, whereas
- five different standard rallies used randomly provides 120 different variations

A little out of position but very skilful.

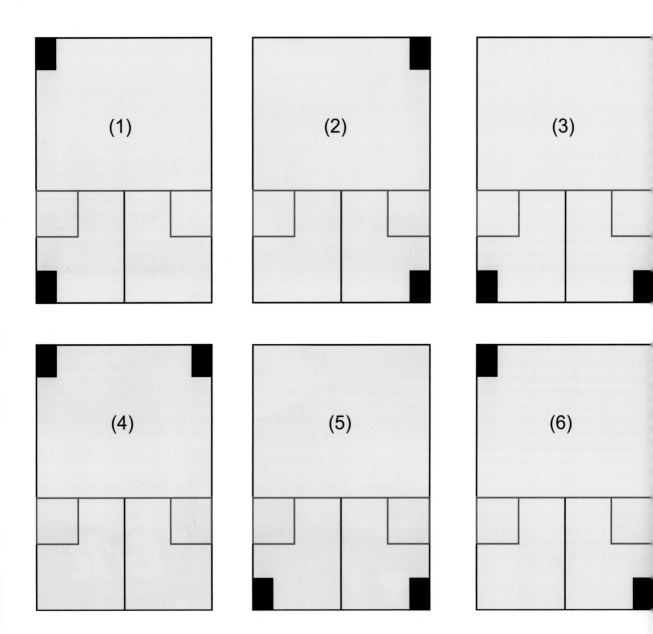

Six examples of standard tactics. (1) backhand wall either short or long; (2) forehand wall either short or long; (3) back backhand or back forehand; (4) front backhand or front forehand; (5) back backhand or front forehand; (6) back forehand or front backhand.

six different standard rallies used randomly provides 720 different variations
seven different standard rallies used randomly provides 5,040 different variations
eight different standard rallies used randomly provides 40,320 different variations
nine different standard rallies used randomly provides 362,880 different variations and so on.

Should you use only one tactic then opponents will very quickly work out where you are putting the ball and therefore take advantage.

This ever changing of tactical ploys that you have worked on and practised over time makes it very difficult for your opponent and allows you to retain the advantage.

In between each rally decide which tactic you will employ for the next rally. Provided that you employ all six

totally at random it will have the effect of:

- keeping your opponent guessing what you are going to do next
- making your opponent overload their reading and decision-making skills
- reducing your opponent's time
- creating more opportunities for you to hit winners
- forcing your opponent to cover more ground.

ose to the end. Strive to apply pressure on your opponent to force them out of position.

PRACTICE AND REFINING

In the context of squash, practice can be described as 'a repeated performance of an exercise with the specific purpose of acquiring a level of proficiency.' To gain the maximum benefit from practice, a number of guidelines need to be observed.

- Practice needs to be in the context of how squash is judged, which is obviously in a game situation. Therefore if it happens in a match, then practise it. If it doesn't happen in a match, it will be of no value!
- Practise the whole skill, in other words rallies, *not* just striking.
- To gain maximum benefit from practice, players need to monitor and evaluate their practice against clearly defined outcomes.
- Full concentration and focus are a must for the duration of the practice. Quality counts! Quality practice teaches you to read your opponent's actions, predict where they are going to hit the ball and to make good tactical decisions.
- Learn to stretch yourself in practice. Practise the areas of your game that will give you the most benefit, not just what you do best.
- Invest your time and energy into quality practice. The experts say that it takes up to 10,000 hours of on-court quality time to become an expert player!
- Become your own coach and study good players to see and recognize patterns of play, and process the information in a meaningful manner. Good players can isolate the visual cues before their opponent strikes the ball, reading the situation and

summing up the probabilities. Observe how they engineer rallies for the best tactical advantage, and try to predict where they will apply pressure. Lesser players watch the ball more, making them reactive, while good players look for the pattern, which makes them anticipatory.

- Practise and play practice matches at three levels. 1. Above your current level to learn new things. 2. At your current level to try to design new tactics. 3. Below your current standard to create more opportunities to practise hitting winners. There is no substitute for practice. Experience really does count!
- Feedback is of major importance during practice. Many coaches provide continuous feedback, offering a comment after each strike of the ball; this is of limited value. It is far better to focus attention on a specific outcome such as a physical target on the court and to be aware of how accurate you are with each shot, making small compensatory adjustments in the racket head angle and direction.

During the learning and practice process, continuously add more shots to the routine so that you restrict your opponent's options and range of stroke, while making it easier to *read* your opponent's actions. Make good *decisions* and increase your range of shots/*actions*. Learn to play the greatest number of variations of shots from all parts of the court, with the maximum degree of disguise, and focus your attention on your opponent's actions as an early warning system.

TOP TIPS FOR PRACTICE

- Random practice – simulating what happens in a game/match situation – is more beneficial than the repetition of practising one shot time after time. Random practice allows players to reproduce the prime elements of rallying – *reading* and *decision making* – which are designed to allow you to predict what your opponent is trying to make the ball do and make good tactical choices for your *action* of striking.
- The more experienced players, through random practice, develop the ability to *recognize patterns of play and tactics* in their opponents and therefore gain an enhanced *awareness of tactical opportunities* that become available. This provides instant feedback that can allow adaptation to occur more readily.
- The greatest benefits are gained from a coach who *guides* you into learning new things by setting problems or asking questions, rather than providing you with all the information to reproduce.

Types of Practice

Routines

To help introduce the development of patterns of play into standard tactical ploys, the following routines will be of great benefit.

Straight Drive with Boast

1 Both players drive the ball to the back of the court, each looking to intercept with an attacking boast (or the volley or off the bounce) when

they are in front of their opponent and/or their opponent is out of position (for example slow coming out of the back corner).

The player retrieving the boast plays a cross-court drive and the attacking player then attempts to volley the cross-court drive straight to the back corner, thus making the opponent travel the full diagonal of the court twice in as many shots.

The practice can be altered by making players hit a straight drive from the boast.

The practice can be progressed by giving players the option of a straight or cross-court drive off the boast.

The practice can be further progressed by giving the players the option of a straight or cross-court drive and a straight or cross-court lob from the back of the court.

The practice can be further progressed by giving the 'retriever' the option of a straight drop off the boast.

The practice can be further progressed by giving the 'retriever' the option of any short shot in response to the boast.

Straight Drive with Drop

Both players drive the ball to the back of the court, each looking to intercept with a volley drop when they are in front of their opponent and/or when their opponent is out of position (for example slow coming out of the back corner).

The player retrieving the drop plays a straight drive, which the attacking player then tries to intercept and volley drive straight back into the back corner, thus making the opponent travel the full length of the court twice in as many shots.

Repeat on the other side of the court.

The practice can be altered by introducing a volley cross-court drop as an alternative shot and then giving the attacking player the option of either a straight or cross-court volley drop.

5   The practice can be further progressed by giving the players the option of a straight or cross-court drive and a straight or cross-court lob from the back of the court.

6   The practice can be further progressed by giving the 'retriever' the option of any short shot in response to the initial short shot.

7   The practice can be further progressed by giving the 'retriever' the option of a straight 'counter' drop off the initial short shot.

Straight and Cross-Court Lob with Boast

1   Both players straight lob the ball into the back corner, each looking to intercept with a volley boast when they are in front of their opponent and/or when their opponent is out of position (for example slow coming out of the back corner).

2   The player retrieving the boast plays a cross-court lob, which the attacking player then tries to intercept and volley to the back corner, thus making the opponent travel the full diagonal of the court twice in as many shots.

3   Repeat on the other side of the court.

4   The practice can be altered by making players hit a straight lob from the boast.

5   The practice can be progressed by giving players the option of a straight or cross-court lob off the boast.

6   The practice can be altered by introducing a volley cross-court drop as an alternative shot to the boast, then further developed by giving the attacking player the option of either a boast or cross-court drop.

7   The practice can be further progressed by giving the players the option of a straight or cross-court drive and a straight or cross-court lob from the back of the court.

8   The practice can be further progressed by giving the 'retriever' the option of a straight drop off the boast.

9   The practice can be further progressed by giving the 'retriever' the option of any short shot in response to the boast.

This is a simple yet effective approach to developing rallies and essentially an awareness of your opponent. The exercises can be made more difficult by encouraging greater accuracy by using target areas on the floor or front wall. In addition, each practice could begin with a service and each rally could be scored to create more of a 'game feel' to the exercises. When played with a degree of success, these practices are physically tough and, because they encourage good decision making and considerable movement, do not expect rallies to last too long!

Once you have developed a degree of accuracy within the 'simple' combinations above, it is appropriate to progress to more complex practices that combine a greater variation of shots and are more technically, tactically and physically demanding.

Straight Drive with Boast, Drop and Cross-Court Lob

1   Both players straight drive the ball into the back corner, each looking to intercept with a volley boast when they are in front of their opponent and/or when their opponent is out of position (for example slow coming out of the back corner).

2   The player retrieving the boast plays a straight drop, which the attacking player then lobs cross-court into the back corner, thus making his opponent travel the full diagonal of the court twice in as many shots.

3   Repeat on the other side of the court.

4   The practice can be altered by making players hit a straight lob from the drop shot.

5   The practice can be progressed by giving players the option of a straight or cross-court lob off the drop shot.

6   The practice can be altered by introducing a volley cross-court drop as an alternative shot to the boast,

then further developed by giving the attacking player the option of either boast or cross-court drop.

7   The practice can be further progressed by giving the players the option of a straight or cross-court drive and a straight or cross-court lob from the back of the court.

8   The practice can be further progressed by giving the 'retriever' the option of a straight drop or cross-court lob off the boast.

9   The practice can be further progressed by giving the 'retriever' the option of any short shot in response to the boast.

Straight Drive with Straight or Cross-Court Volley Drop

1   Both players straight drive the ball into the back corner, each looking to intercept with either a straight or cross-court volley drop when they are in front of their opponent and/or when their opponent is out of position (for example slow coming out of the back corner).

2   The player retrieving the drop plays a straight or cross-court drive, which the attacking player then straight drives into the back corner, thus making his opponent travel the full diagonal/length of the court twice in as many shots.

3   The practice can be further progressed by giving the players the option of a straight or cross-court drive and a straight or cross-court lob from the back of the court.

4   The practice can be further progressed by giving the 'retriever' the option of any short shot in response to the initial short shot.

In Front and Behind

1   Both players drive the ball into the back corner, each looking to intercept with any shot to the front of the court (straight or cross-court) when they are in front of their opponent and/or when their opponent is out of position (for

example slow coming out of the back corner).

2   The player retrieving the short shot plays a straight or cross-court drive or lob, which the attacking player then straight or cross-court drives or lobs to the back of the court.

3   The practice can be developed by introducing a counter drop off the initial short shot or by simply allowing the option of a counter drop if it is perceived as the 'right' shot.

4   The practice can be progressed by introducing a cross-court drive or lob from the back of the court.

5   The practice can be further progressed by giving the 'retriever' the option of any short shot in response to the initial short shot.

Conditioned Games

The purpose of conditioned games is to simulate various aspects of rallies in a game situation. This greatly assists the development of the patterns of play that exist in a match situation, creating a better tactical awareness of how to apply pressure on an opponent through variation of pace, height and placement. Conditioned games teach you to recognize when you have created an advantage and have the opportunity to try for a winning shot.

Sidewall Games

In sidewall games only one side of the court is used, normally distinguished by an extension of the centre line to the front wall. Normally the game would be restricted to backhand or forehand shots with as much variation of pace, length and height as possible, in an attempt to force your opponent to make a mistake. A major benefit of this conditioned game is

that it teaches both players the etiquette of moving around one's opponent so as not to impede their chosen shots.

Back-Court Game

The players are only allowed to hit the ball to the back of the court behind the service line. Normally the ball should strike the front wall above the service line and below the out-line at the top. Again, a wide range of backhand and forehand shots must be applied along with maximum variation of pace and placement.

TOP TIPS

- Force yourself to recover to the T-zone after each shot
- Focus on your opponent's racket action before their point of contact.

Cross-Court Game

Shots can be regarded as loose, allowing your opponent to gain advantage from a ball travelling close to the T-zone. This allows your opponent to take the ball early with a minimum of movement with, for example, a volley drop. Great care must be taken to accurately play the ball around your opponent, who may be placed on or around the T-zone. Best use of height and width is essential.

TOP TIP

- Focus on getting variation of pace and placement away from the T-zone.

Doubles

Each pair rather than the individual must play the ball alternately. It is normal for either pair to take either forehand or backhand exclusively or even to change sides, for example when serving. Played for practice, doubles is ideal for teaching great tactical play, developing accuracy, and

---

TOP TIP

- Look for every opportunity to play short to put your opponent under pressure.

The Recovery (Red) Zone

Aim for this area when you are under pressure or to slow the game down and give you time to recover back to the T-zone. It can also be used to turn defence into attack; using the lob can move your opponent away from the T-zone to give you the opportunity to regain control and look to attack your opponent's return. Shots recommended to play into the red zone are:

• service
• straight or cross-court lob
• volley lob.

The amber zone is best used to consolidate your position during the rally. The red and green zones overlap the amber zone, for example an attacking volley to length could be hit into the amber zone, as could a high lob to length. Use the green zone when you're looking to attack your opponent and apply additional pressure. This target area is suitable for all attacking shots including:

• attacking length drives
• drive and volley drives
• volley kills
• drops and volley drops
• attacking boasts.

Traffic Light Solo Practice

• 90sec – continuous shots into the red zone (point for every shot that hits the red zone then lands behind the service box and inside the service box width)
• 90sec – continuous shots into the amber zone (point for every shot that hits the amber zone then lands at the back of the service box and inside the service box width)
• 90sec – continuous shots into the green zone (point for every shot that hits the green zone then lands behind the short line and inside the service box width)
• 90sec – alternate green zone and red zone (count how many consecutive shots land in the targets, as set out above)

moving around opposing players with less running as each player is essentially only covering half of the court at any one time.
Played socially and for fun, it is one of the most enjoyable squash games, and often includes raucous laughter and much well-humoured banter.

One vs Two

This is one of the best practice situations for developing a *will to win* as opposed to *trying not to lose* attitude. The emphasis falls on the 'one' trying to be positive towards winning the rally, as the chances of one player out-running two players who are only covering half the court are quite remote, even when they are of lesser ability. Should the mindset of the 'one' be to dig in for long rallies then the game will take longer and the 'one' can run themselves ragged very quickly.

Match Practice

As mentioned earlier, the best learning environments for squash are:

coaching, where information is passed, new things are learned and good feedback offered
practice, where the player does his homework, honing the wide range of skills required, and
competition, where all the skills and attributes come together to produce good performances.

Competition is great, whether it is in friendly practice matches or in a championship final, for developing the employment and deployment of good tactics in search of a good result.

Traffic Lights System

The traffic light is a tactical system to develop and improve shot selection using varying heights on the front wall. It encourages players of all levels to use a variety of height and pace to upset an opponent's rhythm and manoeuvre them out of position.

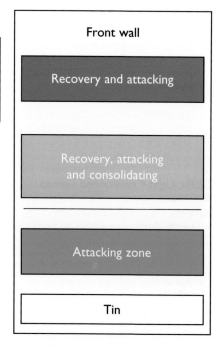

Front wall
Recovery and attacking
Recovery, attacking and consolidating
Attacking zone
Tin

The traffic lights system.

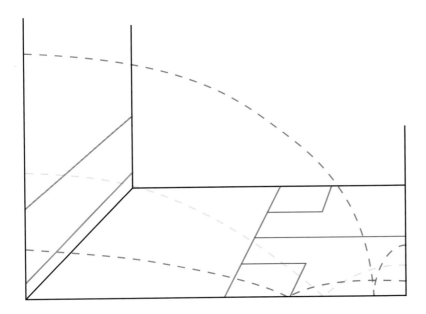

Example of a length using the traffic lights system.

- 90sec – two green zone and one red zone (count how many consecutive shots land in the targets, as set out above)
- 90sec – two red zone and one green zone (count how many consecutive shots land in the targets, as set out above).

The length and width targets will depend on your ability, for example if you find the width targets above too difficult, use the whole back quarter. If the width target is too easy, use half the service box width. (Keep a record of your score and try to improve next time you practise.)

Pairs/Group Traffic Light Practice

Number of targets to achieve in timed challenge or set number. Vary size of targets depending on ability in each practice.

- straight length rally, both players hit red zone only
- straight length rally, both players hit amber zone only

- straight length rally, both players hit green zone only
- straight length rally, player A hits red zone only, player B hits green zone only
- straight length rally, player A hits red zone only, player B can use the whole front wall
- straight length rally, player A hits amber zone only, player B can use the whole front wall
- straight length rally, player A hits green zone only, player B can use the whole front wall.

Traffic Light Conditioned Games

Play PAR scoring to 11, two clear points at 10 all.

Length Game – straight or cross-court with all shots to land behind the short line.

- Player A plays length only and above the service line (red and amber zone only) with one attacking shot per rally (green zone), player B hits below the service line (green zone) with one shot above the service line (red and amber zone)

- Player A plays length only and above the service line (red and amber zone only) with one attacking shot per rally (green zone), player B can play normal game
- Player A hits below the service line (green zone) with one shot above the service line (red zone), player B can play normal game
- Player A plays cross-court lobs and straight drops or volley drops only, player B can play normal game
- Player A plays any straight shot only, player B can play normal game
- Player A plays any cross-court and boasts only, player B can play normal game
- Player A plays back left quarter and front right quarter only, player B can play normal game
- Player A plays back right quarter and front left quarter only, player B can play normal game
- Player A hits only below the service line (green), B plays normal game.

Match Analysis and Fault Diagnosis

Match analysis is a systematic study to determine the cause and essential features of a problematic situation. All too often developing players become disillusioned if their rate of improvement slows down or appears to stagnate. When they feel that many areas of their game need further improvement, where do they start? The answer is often very simple. The principle *read – decision – action* works to identify what to work on and in what order.

If the answer to each question is *yes*, then celebrate, because you will be an exceptionally good player! If you have a number of *no's*, then work on the lowest number first, working in a chronological order. This will begin to resolve the root cause of any problems, rather than working on the symptoms. Next start the process of rectifying the cause of the problem(s) and begin a new regime of practice.

FAULT DIAGNOSIS

Question	Yes	No	If no, tips
Is my start position on the T-zone?			Be on the T-zone
Is my attention focused on my opponent's racket head immediately before they make contact with the ball?			Try to read my opponent's racket action and anticipate where they are going to hit the ball
Am I tracking the ball?			Predict where the ball is going
Am I moving into the striking zone?			Get off the mark quickly and start to raise the racket in preparation
Have I made a shot and target selection?			Make an early choice of target and shot
Am I balanced to strike the ball?			Establish a stable position
Am I using all the joints of my body in sequence?			Keep the body relaxed and in rhythm
Am I hitting the ball in my striking zone?			Keep a loose grip and strike the ball equal distance from the tip of each shoulder
Have I a relaxed follow-through?			Use the momentum of the follow-through to assist my recovery
Am I getting back to the T-zone?			Get off the ball as fast as possible

Rally Ending Analysis

Use the diagram on page 85, together with the table opposite, to depict the outcome of rallies.

Instructions

When a player hits a winner, draw 'O' at the point where the ball was hit. When a player hits an error, draw 'X' at the point where the ball was hit. Use different coloured pens if possible.

Response to a Short Shot

Instructions

To notate player A. When player B hits a short shot (in front of the short line) write 'X' at the point where the ball hit by player A lands. If an error, write 'XE'; if a winner write 'XW'. If player B hits a winner write 'W'. If player B volleys the return from player A, write 'V' where the volley was played.

Response to a Length

Instructions

To notate player A. When player B hits a shot past the back of the line behind the service box, write 'X' at the point where the ball played by player A lands. If an error write 'XE'; if a winner write 'XW'. If the length by player B is a winner, write 'W'. If player B volleys the return by player A, write 'V' where the volley was made. If player A volleys a shot that would have been a length, write 'VB' where the ball bounces (or 'VXE' or 'VXW' as appropriate).

MATCH EVALUATION SHEET

Which two aspects of the match were you most happy with?

1.

2.

Which features of the match were you least happy with?

1.

2.

Your opponent's:

Strengths

Weaknesses

How would you play this person again?

RALLY ENDING ANALYSIS

Position

1	2	3	4
5	6	7	8
9	10	11	12
13	14	15	16

Enter the number of shots in a rally, the outcome – winner (W), error (E), let (L), stroke (S) – the player's initials that played the shot, the shot played and the position the shot was played on court using the codes below.

Shot

D – drive	V – volley
B – boast	C – cross-court
D – drop	S – serve
L – lob	K – kill

Player A .... vs Player B ....

Rally	Shots	Outcome	Player	Shot	Position
1					
2					
3					
4					
5					
6					
7					
8					
9					
10					
11					
12					
13					
14					
15					
16					
17					
18					
19					
20					
21					
22					
23					
24					
25					
26					
27					
28					
29					
30					
31					
32					

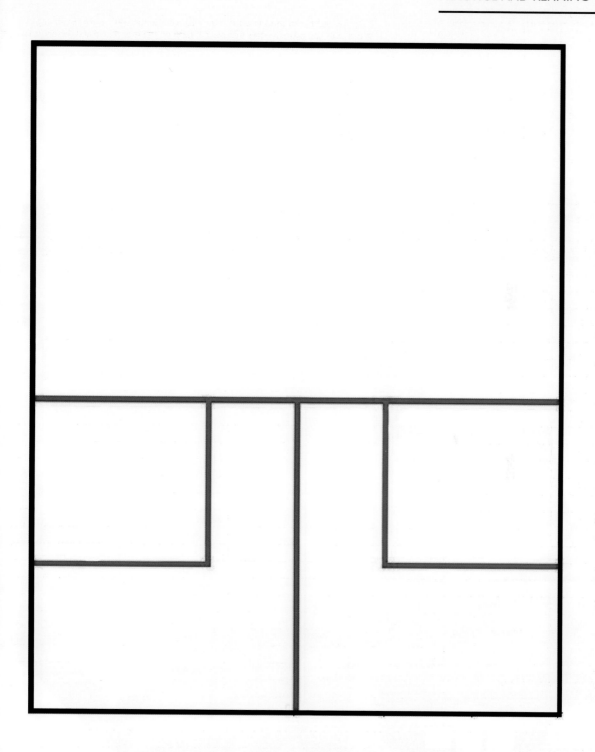

quash court aerial view. Use this diagram to indicate (a) response to a short shot and (b) response to length.

PART III

FITNESS AND MENTAL TOUGHNESS

CHAPTER 12

ENERGY SYSTEMS AND THE PHYSICAL DEMANDS OF SQUASH

Many factors contribute to how players play and compete in squash. Skill, mental toughness and fitness are the most important. Squash players that have the stamina to keep playing for longer, especially into that vital deciding game, have a better track record. By physical fitness I mean the overall condition of each individual player. Squash players tend to be towards the upper echelons of physical fitness, dependent on how much quality training they undertake. These factors must come together in the correct balance and ratio to deliver the best results in open competition.

Squash is a physically demanding sport and one that contributes greatly to overall health and wellbeing. Fitness is specific to each individual sport, and squash, being a sport made up of a series of rallies, can go on for extended periods of time with limited periods for rest. It is a sport that requires high intensity bouts of vigorous physical activity.

At times, *anaerobic respiration* (the production of energy without oxygen) is required for short bursts of effort. More often players will respire *aerobically* (the production of energy with oxygen). This is the most effective way to work. Other important factors are a player's *speed*, which incorporates the ability to use a wide range of movement; *flexibility*, which uses large amounts of force; *strength*; *endurance*; and *percentage body fat*. Squash embraces all these components, and they require appropriate training.

The three energy systems are discussed below.

1 The *phosphate energy system*, used for immediate high intensity work lasting only 5 to 15sec, does not require oxygen as a delivery system. It is the key supplier for high intensity work. Agility and speed training are best for developing the phosphate energy system, as they prepare the body to convert phosphates quickly and work at a high level of intensity for longer periods.

2 The *anaerobic energy system* is the process of releasing energy from food in the form of glucose without the presence of oxygen. Blood can only be delivered to a muscle if it is relaxed, therefore when it is tensed for long periods of time, such as during a game of squash, the cells begin to respire within the anaerobic threshold. The fuel from this energy system is produced quickly but is short lived, lasting 1.5 to 3min, producing lactic acid waste which causes fatigue in the form of muscle pain. The oxygen debt from this process also triggers faster breathing. Training to build anaerobic capacity prepares the body to increase the level of enzymes that convert carbohydrate into energy. This makes the body more tolerant to lactic acid, which causes fatigue.

3 The *aerobic energy system* provides longer-term energy and requires sufficient oxygen for the process to take place. If the body is able to process enough oxygen it will respire aerobically. In this case oxygen is combined with glucose, which results in energy being produced. The waste products are water and carbon dioxide; this form of respiration is much more efficient than anaerobic respiration.

Oxygen Transport

Every living cell of the body requires oxygen; the body is unable to operate without it. Sitting at home reading this book your body will require approximately half a litre of oxygen each time that you inhale. However, when playing a hard game of squash the need for oxygen will increase considerably to approximately three litres – slightly less for women – which is about half of what the lungs are capable of inhaling. The physical demands of squash mean that the oxygen supply can become, and often is, severely depleted. The body can make up for the shortfall through anaerobic respiration, but the delivery system has to work harder for it to function. This causes the body to slow down and eventually stop. Rest is required for the body to replenish the shortfall and start respiring aerobically again. The body, through training, can adapt and become more efficient in the way it responds to the need for oxygen.

The process starts when the lungs, acting like sponges, extract oxygen from the atmosphere and expel carbon dioxide from the body. They operate in the sealed environment of the chest cavity, reacting to the diaphragm contracting and relaxing. The oxygen is carried in the blood, which flows around the body to provide oxygen and nutrients to the muscle cells and to help remove waste. To move the oxygenated blood around the body to the muscles, an engine is required, in this case the heart. The heart pumps the blood around the body through arteries and veins. As a general rule, arteries operate at high pressure, carrying oxygenated blood away from the heart to the cells; the veins operate at a lower pressure, carrying deoxygenated blood back to the heart.

The blood flows through the body via either the pulmonary or systemic pathway. The pulmonary circulation carries deoxygenated blood from the right atrium to the right ventricle and through the pulmonary artery to the lungs where it becomes oxygenated in the capillaries. The blood then flows through the pulmonary vein to the left atrium and then the left ventricle. The systemic circulation carries oxygenated blood from the left ventricle to all the cells of the body, initially through the aorta. The systematic capillaries allow the exchange of oxygen and the deoxygenated blood flows back to the right atrium. The blood also helps with the removal of waste products. The amount of oxygen used at rest will be approximately fifty per cent and during a hard game of squash this percentage will decrease dependent on the level of fitness.

Here, rather than consult the referees, David Palmer (in white) struggles to get a clear run to the ball.

CHAPTER 13

TESTING FOR FITNESS

Fitness testing or monitoring provides players with vital information about their physical condition. A current position needs to be worked out as a start point, before serious training can begin with safety. Over the years, accurate field testing has proved to be reliable without the need for expensive equipment, which can restrict the degree of specificity when testing for squash as opposed to other sports. Fitness for squash is different from fitness for swimming or football, for example.

Multi-Stage Fitness Test (Bleep Test)

The bleep test is a shuttle run test to measure players' aerobic fitness (which is the player's ability to take in and use oxygen). Squash is a very aerobic sport; the rallies are often long and recovery periods between rallies are relatively short, which means that elite players must have very good aerobic fitness.

The test requires that players run between two markers twenty metres apart to maintain a specific series of timed beeps, starting with an easy rhythm and intensity. Progressively, the time allocated between beeps is reduced to reach the required twenty-metre marker. When the player fails to reach the allocated marker on three successive beeps he withdraws and a calculation is made of how many successful runs have been achieved. This is then recorded to provide a valid measurement. Provided that the same protocols are achieved and maintained at each test, any training effect can be measured over time.

Testing for Endurance

Players can improve their base level endurance fitness by:

- Running 20/30/40min × 3 times per week (depending on age) to set targets. For example, how many times can the player run around the park in 30min? At the start of the off season the player might be able to do three laps of the park and by the end of the summer they may be able to manage almost four
- Sets of 20 court sprints: 6 × 20 court sprints in under 1min with 30sec rest. (The player should aim to do the same time for each set)
- 50 or 100 court sprints: 2 × 50 court sprints in under 2min 30sec with 90sec rest (the rest time can be reduced as the player gets stronger) or 1 × 100 court sprints in under 5min
- Pyramid runs: in pairs, 1 × 10 court sprints then partner, 1 × 20 court sprints then partner, 1 × 30 court sprints then partner, 1 × 40 court sprints then partner, 1 × 50 court sprints then partner, then 40, 30, 20 and 10 (the target number can change depending on age and fitness)
- Pyramid runs: in pairs, 6 sets of 2 court sprints then partner, 4 sets of 3 court sprints then partner, 2 sets of 6 court sprints, 1 set of 12 court sprints then partner, 2 sets of 6 court sprints then partner, 4 sets of 3 court sprints and 6 sets of 2 court sprints
- Rowing: 1000m or 2000m (most gyms will have a Concept 2 rowing machine). Set targets. For example, how long does it take to row 1000m? At the start of the summer a player might be able to complete the target in 5min; by the end of the summer they may have reduced this time to 4min 20sec.
- Rowing sprints: 10 × 200m (set time targets with coach or trainer),

---

AVERAGE BLEEP TEST ATTAINMENT LEVELS

Age	Gender	Bleep test measure	Age	Gender	Bleep test measure
14	Female	12.0	14	Male	13.8
16	Female	12.1	16	Male	14.5
18	Female	13.3	18	Male	15.0
Senior	Female	13.8	Senior	Male	15.4

Note: These averages are approximate values. They are provided to give players a guide to the scores they could be achieving but do not take into account individual differences in rates of physical development. Your scores should be compared to these values and then discussed with your coach to identify the key focus of your physical training programme.

45sec rest after each set. (The player should aim to do the same time for each set).

Test 1 for Speed and Agility: The 16 Corner Challenge

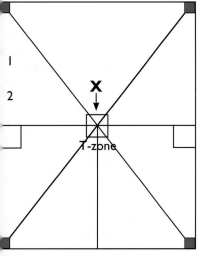

The idea is to move, run, lunge, twist and turn as fast as possible, by going four times round the corners of the court and moving back to the T-zone (the T-zone is roughly one metre from the T all the way round) after each corner has been touched. Players should aim to achieve a personal best time (PB) on each occasion they attempt the 16 Corner Challenge. Players must move in the order shown below. If a player makes an error they must start again.

1   The coach stands on 'X', keeps the time and directs the player
2   When the coach says go, the stopwatch begins and the player sprints towards corner no. 1
3   The player lunges and touches the target placed in the corner on the floor
4   The player must move as fast as possible backwards and must put one foot into the T-zone as marked out left
5   The player then sprints to corner no. 2, lunges and touches the target on the floor

6   The player must then move backwards and put one foot into the T-zone
7   As the player approaches the T-zone he turns and runs towards corner no. 3, then lunges, touches the target on the floor, turns and sprints forward and puts one foot into the T-zone
8   The player then turns to corner no. 4, lunges and touches the target on the floor
9   The player then turns and puts one foot into the T-zone, then continues to corner no. 1
10 Four circuits of the court are required when attempting the 16 Corner Challenge. After you have touched the sixth corner sprint forward past the 'T' and stop the watch. Keep a record of your personal best time.

Test 2 for Speed and Agility

Players can improve their speed and agility by:

TESTING FOR SPEED AND AGILITY

Age	Gender	Corners	Time (sec)	Age	Gender	Corners	Time (sec)
14	Female	4	13	14	Male	4	12
		8	26			8	24
		16	55			16	48
16	Female	4	12.5	16	Male	4	11.5
		8	24			8	22
		16	53			16	44
18	Female	4	12	18	Male	4	10.5
		8	24			8	21
		16	51			16	42
Senior	Female	4	11	Senior	Male	4	10
		8	23			8	20
		16	48			16	41

Note: These averages are approximate values. They are provided to give players a guide to the scores they could be achieving but do not take into account individual differences in rates of physical development. Your scores should be compared to these values and then discussed with your coach to identify the key focus of your physical training programme.

- 10 × 20sec speed ghosting, which is using realistic squash movement patterns without a ball: 1 step off the T-zone, 20sec rest after each set
- 10 × 30sec speed ghosting: 2 steps from the T-zone, 30sec rest after each set
- 10 × 12 shots full court speed ghosting: 30sec rest after each set
- Skipping: 10 × 1min skipping; set a target for the number of skips, a good aim would be 100 in 1min); 45sec rest after each set
- Squash court shuttle runs: 10 × 30sec shuttles. Starting on the back wall, sprint to and touch the back of the service box with your hand, then back and touch the back wall, then sprint to and touch the short line, then back and touch the back wall, then sprint to and touch the line set by the coach halfway between the short line and front wall, then back and touch the back wall, then sprint to and touch the front wall, then back and touch the back wall; repeat for 30sec. Aim to finish at the same place for each set. As strength is gained over time players will start to finish further on.

TESTING FOR STAMINA (TEST 1)

Age	Gender	Length of run (km)	Average times
13/14	Male	1	5min
		3	15min
		5	25min
16	Male	1	4min 20sec
		3	13min
		5	21min 40sec

TESTING FOR STAMINA (TEST 2)

Age	Gender	Time
13/14	Male	59sec/1min per set
16	Male	57/58sec per set
18	Male	56/57sec per set
Senior	Male	55sec per set

Testing for Stamina

Test 1: Long Runs

Completing a 3km run per week will help build stamina. Do not panic if you are not reaching the average time targets as listed, just keep working. If, on the other hand, you are easily achieving these targets, speak to your coach who will help you re-adjust your times. The key here is to push yourself, don't hold back!

Test 2: Sets of 20 Court Length Sprints

Ten sets of twenty court length sprints; after each set have 1min rest then repeat; each set should take the same time. Lower your recovery time as you improve.

CHAPTER 14

GUIDELINES FOR TRAINING

Warm-Ups

The importance of a good warm-up has never been in doubt. The purpose of a warm-up is to prepare the body to compete, practice or train, which requires that the body be warm, with the heart rate and lungs working at or close to the levels they are required to work at during the match. It also provides a mental warm-up and ensures concentration levels and focus of attention commensurate for the match, alongside all the prepared techniques, skills and specific movement patterns. A good warm-up, as well as preparing the body and mind to compete or train, will help guard against injury and should precede all games, practice and training sessions.

The ideal warm-up for squash requires a steady increase of aerobic activity. This can be done off court, beginning with some light jogging, building in intensity, followed by stretching and racket work on court. Alternatively, the warm-up can start on court with some easy rhythmical routines with a ball, either alone or with a partner. This should build to some open rallies using the specific skills of reading and shot selection, and the actions of movement and striking at the speed and intensity required during the match.

Cool-Downs

A normal response for some squash players after a game is to slump in the changing room, elbows on knees with the head bowed. Nothing could be worse! After a game of squash or a training session, a cool-down period is advised. This is to facilitate the body to lose excess heat, to help the process of flushing out lactic acid (produced as the waste product from activity) and to allow the body to reach a relaxed resting state.

Some form of low-level aerobic activity is advised. This could be slow rhythmic movement, for example on court striking a ball gently, followed by some stretching. The stretching can either be static or take a slow rhythmic movement. Stretching the muscles to full length has the effect of flushing the lactic acid and aids the recovery process. A healthy muscle is usually long and thin.

For the more serious player, an additional stage of recovery can be undertaken with ice baths for the lower limbs for up to 10min maximum, alternating cold shower (30sec) and warm (2 to 3min) for three to four cycles and nutrition/hydration (bananas before the shower, and carbohydrate/replacement drinks).

Specificity

Training programmes should be specific to squash. If you cycle 30 miles a day to and from work it will help by providing a base level of fitness on which to build for the demands of squash but won't be sufficient by itself.

Adaptation will only occur to the movement patterns performed in training. These movement patterns should reflect the specific movements and work the muscle groups that are used in squash.

Individuality

Everyone is different in their physical make up and will respond very differently to training programmes. Young developing

COMPONENTS OF FITNESS					
Training	Strength	Speed	Power	Aerobic	Anaerobic
Long steady runs				Y	
Sprinting 10sec, long rests		Y			
Interval training 1–90sec					Y
Interval training 1–3min				Y	
Hill running	Y				Y
Circuit training	Y	Y	Y		
Plyometric training	Y	Y	Y		
Light weights	Y				
Heavy weights	Y	Y	Y		

squash players should adhere to the principles of LTAD as discussed earlier.

Overload

The body must be made to work harder
than at rest. Remember the FIT acronym:

* *frequency* – train often enough with
  suitable rest periods with a high level
  of
* *intensity* – close to your threshold for
  the right length of
* *time* – for long enough to allow your
  body to adapt to a training programme.

Adaptation occurs when bodily changes
occur due to changes in demand. A period
of recovery allows the body time to rest
and prepare to train again. Programmes
need planning to allow time for the training regime to take effect, with progression to increase training loads slowly. It
is important to increase the amount and
intensity of training at a gradual pace
because injury can cause lengthy lay-offs
leading to reversibility if training stops.

The table on page 93 links training to
the components of fitness.

The joy of victory.

CHAPTER 15

PLANNING FOR FITNESS

In squash a performance plan is a process of actions to bring about specific outcomes that enhance results in competition. To achieve the maximum benefit from any training plan there should be a careful balance of *competition, skill building and training,* the components divided into separate training periods, each with a different emphasis to promote optimal progress.

Each training period should be designed with specific targets and emphasis that encompass the different components, which will include loading, repetitions recovery periods etc.

Structure of the Plan

The plan is divided into three phases:

> *preparation* – pre season when the build up starts
> *competition* – in season, which is the business phase
> *active rest* – off season, recovery and recuperation.

The basic building block of any training programme is usually of one week duration and is called a *micro-cycle.* A micro-cycle is made up of:

> six- and one-day periods
> five- and two-day periods
> four- and three-day periods.

The latter numbers of days are rest periods. An example of a micro-cycle: a light skill building workout is a practice routine from one corner, while a medium skill building workout is a routine from two corners and a heavy skill building workout is a routine from three corners. The first table opposite shows a micro-cycle with skill building work.

MICRO-CYCLE SKILL BUILDER						
Monday	**Tuesday**	**Wednesday**	**Thursday**	**Friday**	**Saturday**	**Sunday**
Light	Medium	Medium	Heavy	Medium	Light	Rest

MICRO-CYCLE CONDITIONING						
Monday	**Tuesday**	**Wednesday**	**Thursday**	**Friday**	**Saturday**	**Sunday**
Sprints		Sprints		Sprints		Rest

MICRO-CYCLE RESISTANCE						
Monday	**Tuesday**	**Wednesday**	**Thursday**	**Friday**	**Saturday**	**Sunday**
	Strength		Strength		Strength	Rest

To include conditioning training, we could insert sessions on three days a week. So the plan is further expanded as shown in the second table above.

To include resistance training, we could include it on the days we are not conditioning training (third table above and table overleaf).

Once the micro-cycle has been planned, we can arrange daily sessions for each day of the week, except for rest days, which in the example below would be Sunday.

For example, the Wednesday session plan could take the following structure:

10:00	warm-up
10:15	skill building
10:45	competitive game
11:15	sprint-recovery training
11:45	cool-down and review session.

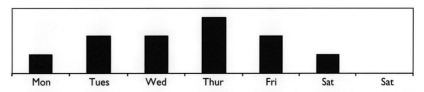

The micro-cycle.

FULL MICRO-CYCLE							
	Monday	**Tuesday**	**Wednesday**	**Thursday**	**Friday**	**Saturday**	**Sunday**
Skill building	Light	Medium	Medium	Heavy	Medium	Light	Rest
Condition	Sprints		Sprints		Sprints		
Strength		Resistance		Resistance		Resistance	

The player should continue to build micro-cycles, varying the daily session according to the phase of the plan to include:

- the work effort – whether extensive or intensive
- the skill building and tactical requirements.

This should also incorporate the necessary rest and recovery periods to avoid overtraining. Training should be varied to maintain motivation.

Players may gather micro-cycles into meso-cycles of two to four months' duration if the overall goal or phase of the training scheme has been determined. That is, the different phases of the annual plan when general preparation, squash-specific preparation, pre-competition, competition and tapering off are considered.

Flexibility is the key factor in preparing training plans, and most players recognize that they can only plan micro-cycles in daily detail two or three weeks into the future. Since it is difficult to predict the adaptive training response of each player, players must take into consideration the ever-changing reactions to training as the plan progresses. It is essential that players be aware of the overall guidelines within which the appropriate training takes place. This often takes the form of broadly described meso-cycles, where the specific details are left blank. If each block represents a micro-cycle and its size indicates its work volume and/or intensity, then a nine-week meso-cycle could take the shape of that shown in the graph above right.

The overall pattern would be an undulating level of work with an overall increase in conditioning and squash-specific skill

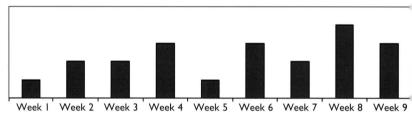

The meso-cycle.

building. Likewise, a two-month general preparation phase and a two-month squash-specific phase might resemble the graph shown below.

This would be appropriate when the overall conditioned state of the player is increasing month by month as a result of judicious training. As the volume of training increases and the player's condition increases, the volume of training is increased even more, and so on, until a point is reached where the incremental improvements through volume training become slight to non-existent.

If the first and second months are the general preparation phase, the emphasis will be on the volume of work to build aerobic and muscular endurance. As

TOP TIPS FOR TRAINING PROGRAMMES

- Design a plan – it is best to work this through with your coach or fitness professional
- Be realistic with your time commitment
- Build in your competition programme
- Include your results in competition in the monitoring of your training
- Quality is best – avoid overtraining.

progress is made on general endurance conditioning, the player will have to make a decision as to when and how much intensity to introduce and how much volume.

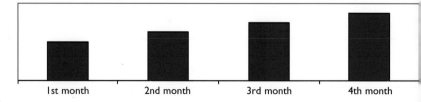

A four-month meso-cycle.

CHAPTER 16

TRAINING FOR CORE STABILITY

As discussed briefly on page 53 (Chapter 6), *core stability* is essential to good squash performance as it directly links the processes of moving into position, the striking action of the ball and recovery back to the T-zone. All squash players will have experienced some form of lower back discomfort, most instances of which are likely to have been alleviated with a greater level of strength, stability and flexibility in the middle regions of the body.

For the serious squash player who does not have the time to make regular trips to the gym or the resources to engage a personal trainer, a small investment in a *swiss ball* and a minimum of one hour per week in three lots of 20min could alleviate a high percentage of core stability issues and make you a better squash player. This could easily be interspersed with circuit training to develop strength and speed and some plyometric exercises designed specifically for squash movement patterns.

Core stability exercises can be done as stand-alone exercises at home or as you cool down after a friendly game, match or training session. The objective is to perform each exercise *slowly* and with good concentration, focusing on isolating and working the middle regions while maintaining balance throughout. Many of the exercises can be adapted to work on a mat as well as with a ball.

Start a session with three simple exercises to help stabilize muscles before progressing to slow movement. Each of the first three exercises should involve contracting the stomach muscles and holding for a count of ten before repeating or changing.

Three simple core stability/strength exercises.

The following six exercises should be done *as slowly as possible* with the emphasis being on control of the muscles, clear focus on maintaining balance and good concentration.

1.   Roll (right above and below)

Kneeling behind the ball with arms outstretched, hands at the top of the ball and maintaining a straight back, gently roll the ball away from you until your body is at full extension; hold for a count of four and slowly return to the start position.

2.   Straight Arm Sit-Up (below)

With your back arched on the ball and your arms extended, slowly lift your shoulder blades off the ball and reach for the ceiling; hold for a count of four and slowly return to the start position.

3. Reverse Sit-Up (above)

Lie on the floor holding the ball between your legs and heels. Slowly bring your knees towards your chest, hold for a count of four and slowly return to the start position.

4. Backwards Leg Lifts (above and right)

With your hands and feet on the floor, lie on the ball. Slowly raise your legs so that your feet are above the level of your head; hold for a count of four and slowly return to the start position.

5. Reverse Leg Lift (above and right)

Lay in a press-up position with your feet on the ball, your hands on the floor and your elbows at 90 degrees. While slowly pushing with your arms, raise one leg as high as possible and hold for a count of four. Repeat with the opposite leg.

6. The Bridge (left)

Form a bridge with your feet on the ball and your shoulders and head on the floor. Keeping your body straight, slowly raise one leg to where your thigh is at right angles to your body. Hold for a count of four and lower. Repeat with the other leg.

TRAINING PROGRAMME		
Level 1	novices	1 × 10 repeats
Level 2	intermediate	2 × 10 repeats
Level 3	advanced	2 × 15 repeats

CHAPTER 17

INJURY PREVENTION

Squash is a sport that requires a lot of physical effort and is played in close proximity to one's opponent, making injuries inevitable at some stage. A small rubber ball travelling at great speed can cause severe bruising if a player is caught in the line of fire. The rules and etiquette of squash are very clear and require junior players to wear protective goggles on court to avoid eye injury. The old adage still rings true: 'Prevention is better than a cure.' If players stick to the rules then serious injury is very rare.

Direct contact between two players through a direct collision or being struck by an opponent's racket is the most likely cause of bruising or swelling. Muscle strains can occur and are usually caused by players exerting too much force on their muscles due to lack of ability or fitness. This causes the muscle fibres to tear or separate. Overuse can also cause injury. As the name suggests, overuse is the result of excessive, repetitive movements, which over time cause the muscle or ligament to wear out. The healing process requires changes to the movement pattern, technique or a dramatic reduction in activity. Injuries to tendons and ligaments are usually in the form of inflammation or tears and can take considerable time to heal. Unlike muscles, tendons do not have a blood supply, which lengthens the healing process.

What to Do in the Event of an Injury

In the event of an injury it is essential to carry out an assessment of its severity. Should the injury be deemed serious, such as a broken bone or severed Achilles tendon, the injured person should go to the A&E department. If a serious injury is examined by a medical professional soon after it has occurred, the chance of a quick recovery is increased. Should the injury be less severe, such as a small muscle tear or some soreness, the RICE method is advised (see below).

- **Rest** – stop the activity, especially at the point of pain
- **Ice** – as soon as possible apply ice covered with a towel, as direct contact with ice will burn the skin
- **Compression** – apply compression to the injury; check frequently that any swelling under the compression is not inhibiting blood flow

---

INJURY CAUSES AND REMEDY

Common squash injuries	Likely cause	Likely remedies
Cramps	Dehydration, tiredness and lack of muscular endurance	Stretching to keep the muscle long Hydration with body salt replacement Fitness training regime
Blisters	Ill-fitting footwear, postural problems and poor technique	Well-fitting, proper squash shoes with good support
Joint pains, usually lower back, hips and knees	Poor technique Postural imbalance Overuse	RICE Develop good techniques with economy of movement
Muscle tears and strains	Unusual sudden movement Overuse Overloading Overstretching	RICE Core stability training programme Develop better techniques
Ligament and tendon tears	Unusual sudden movement Overuse Overloading Overstretching	RICE Core stability training programme Develop better techniques

- **Elevation** – try to raise the injured part above the heart as this will reduce throbbing and help drainage.

The key to injury prevention is a well-balanced training programme that includes a high proportion of core stability work linked to the specific movement patterns, techniques and skills of squash. Learn to listen to your body and understand what it is saying to you; rectify any problems with some positive action.

> **TOP TIPS**
>
> - Always seek professional help and advice from a doctor, physiotherapist or health professional
> - Balance your squash playing and training as *quality* time and an investment for longevity
> - Early action is always best – leaving even a small injury for a few days to 'wait and see' can delay recovery.

This picture shows two young players taking part in a national competition. However, good physical preparation reduces the risk of injury at all levels.

CHAPTER 18

NUTRITION FOR TRAINING AND PLAYING

Nutrition is the process of taking in and utilizing food for growth, repair and maintenance of the body. Food is processed through our digestive system to yield energy, which is transported in the blood through the lungs and heart to the muscles in the body.

Food and Fluid

Food and fluid have a major impact on any form of physical activity, particularly high-energy sports such as squash. A squash match can last for well over an hour with a very tense last few minutes, which always prove crucial to the outcome. It is often at this point that tiredness becomes a critical factor. A well-balanced diet, combined with a high fluid intake and appropriate training, will help a player to maintain high energy levels throughout long hard matches and will also stimulate a speedy recovery.

Dehydration is the most likely cause of a poor performance, as it has a detrimental effect on the body's ability to work at its best. A two per cent loss of body fluid reduces energy levels by about twenty per cent. Energy drinks containing approximately six to eight per cent carbohydrate should be taken prior to, during and after exercise to ensure a good performance.

Squash Players' Good Food Guide

Carbohydrates

While maintaining a well-balanced diet and sufficient fluid intake, a player's diet should be sixty to seventy per cent carbohydrate to maintain energy levels and slow the rate of fatigue. Carbohydrate comes in two forms.

1 **Simple (unnatural) carbohydrates** include sucrose (sugar), used in cakes, pastries, chocolate, most soft fizzy drinks and other processed food. These should only supplement your overall carbohydrate intake. It is worth noting the difference between simple natural carbohydrates and unnatural ones. Simple natural carbohydrates occur in most fruit, which contribute to a healthy diet. They release energy slowly. Simple unnatural carbohydrates are quickly and easily broken down into glucose and converted into energy soon after they are consumed. However, this causes blood sugar levels (glucose) to rise rapidly, giving a boost of energy, which is quickly followed by a sharp drop of blood sugar levels and therefore a drop in energy levels, which can ultimately leave you feeling more tired than in the first place.

2 **Complex carbohydrates** include rice, potatoes, pasta, bread and beans and should form the basis of your carbohydrate intake. These food products are broken down at a slower rate causing a steady supply of energy to the body.

Fats

Fats should be consumed in moderation, as the body will normally have adequate stores. Around 20 per cent of the energy in your diet should come from fat. The average fat intake for men is around 100–150 g per day and for women 75–130g, providing 40–45 per cent of the total energy in their diet. This ratio is best reduced to between 20 and 30 per cent per day as an average energy intake. As well as being a source of energy, fats provide vital nutrients that help synthesize compounds and tissues vital to normal body functions. There are two kinds of fats.

Visible Fat
- butter
- margarine
- lard
- fatty meat
- pork crackling
- poultry skin.

Non-Visible Fat
- dark meats: beef, lamb, duck, pork, liver, kidneys
- oily fish: salmon, pilchards, sardines, mackerel
- dark meat products: sausages, pate, pork pies, burgers
- dairy products: full-fat cheeses, cream, whole milk
- potato products: crisps, chips
- all fried food
- olives
- nuts.

Low-Fat Alternatives
- white meat without the skin: chicken/turkey breast
- white fish: cod, haddock , plaice
- shellfish: prawns, dressed crab, mussels, squid
- dairy products: skimmed milk, low-fat cheeses, yoghurt.

Protein

Protein-based food is needed to help repair and grow muscles. Only 10–15 per cent of our energy comes from this

Don't forget the carbohydrate!

An example of a pre-match meal:

- low-fat cheese sandwich on whole-meal bread
- piece of fruit sliced with peanut butter
- wholemeal toast with honey
- tomato juice, unsweetened.

During matches energy levels can be topped up with carbohydrate-rich drinks, which also maintain fluid intake. A squash match can last for over an hour and in warm conditions the body can lose up to two litres of fluid. This means approximately 250ml of water or glucose drinks should be taken between each game in a best-of-five contest.

After the match, the body stores will be depleted of both energy and fluid. These are best replenished with carbohydrate-rich drinks, especially if taken within the first thirty minutes, and further replenished two to three hours later with a carbohydrate-rich meal.

During tournaments or events where more than one round per day has to be played, simple carbohydrate can replace complex carbohydrates, as they are less bulky and more concentrated. Again, carbohydrate drinks can prove ideal as they contain fluid as well as energy.

source, which is normally met easily with a well-balanced diet.

Animal Protein
- meat
- fish
- dairy food
- eggs.

Vegetable Protein
- brown rice (short grain)
- wholemeal pasta
- wholemeal bread
- all vegetables
- nuts/seeds/lentils/pulses.

Pre-match meals should be light and high in complex carbohydrates, and low in fat and protein. Meals should be eaten a good two to three hours prior to the match to have the best effect. Fluid intake, especially fruit juices which are high in minerals and water, must be high to ensure adequate hydration.

TOP TIPS FOR SQUASH NUTRITION

- Regard nutrition as essential to any playing/training regime
- Build in rest days from training and playing to help nutrition have the best effect
- Eat more fresh vegetables and whole-grain food
- Keep your fat intake down
- Drink lots of fluids
- Re-fuel/hydrate during your matches
- Re-fuel immediately you come off-court.

CHAPTER 19

MENTAL TOUGHNESS AND WORKING RELATIONSHIPS

The truly great squash players of all time, without exception, display a mental toughness that pushes them to strive to perfect their skills and attributes. It is this determination and mindset to grow and develop as squash players that motivates them to achieve through searching for good solutions, high-quality focused practice and hard work. Their mental strength allows them to deal with the setbacks of injury and losses, and provides the springboard from which they become winners. The desire and challenge for growth and improvement is as great as the quest for victory – this mental toughness underpins their work ethic and performance.

People are not born with the skills needed to succeed as squash players. These skills and attributes are learned and only come to fruition with the determination and effort to improve through dedicated practice. A winning mentality is something that grows into the ability to work hard together with the determination to improve in the competitive arena. Players who succeed do not rest on the laurels of success or the disappointment of defeat, but constantly analyse their performances and stretch themselves to overcome weaknesses.

Mental toughness is displayed in all champions. It fosters a healthy attitude towards training, practice and learning, and allows players to overcome the many setbacks within competition.

Concentration

Concentration or focus of attention is an essential component of playing squash and is equal in importance to any other skill.

Often players and coaches describe or term this state of concentration as being in the 'zone'. This has been described as when the size of the ball looks the same size as a football, the target the same size as a football pitch and where time seems to be in slow motion. This happens when the player achieves a very high level of attention or focus.

This level of attention does not come with the flick of a switch but builds to a level by applying pressure on one's opponent (see Part II for more detail). It is difficult to hold this level of attention

A clear focus of attention is essential.

indefinitely as the brain needs to rest for short periods. So, rather than flatlining at this peak level of attention, the level of concentration fluctuates slightly in waves as it ebbs and flows. When you understand this process you can learn to accurately predict when the best opportunities will arise to apply most pressure on an opponent and so increase the likelihood to win the most points. As the same process occurs for your opponent, the most beneficial time to apply tactical pressure is when you are at the crest of the concentration wave and your opponent is at the ebb.

In practice and in competition this focus of attention should be applied during rallies as the most beneficial time to rest the brain is between rallies. This level of concentration is best applied by training the brain to follow the steps below between each rally.

1 Regard the last rally as past and finished, in other words do not punish yourself if you have lost the rally or congratulate yourself for winning the point, just be aware that you are unable to change that outcome
2 Rest your brain, take two to three large deep breaths from your diaphragm and relax the whole body to enhance the process of re-oxygenating
3 Decide on a tactical ploy selected from your repertoire of standard tactics
4 Visualize yourself executing a well-placed service or receive, then progressing the rally while being very aware and accurate, and finally winning the rally
5 Execute the rally.

The Final Build-Up to Competition

Two Days Prior
Good players invest a lot of time, money and effort in improving. Preparation is an integral part of this process and will begin months, weeks and days before

a big match or event. This preparation, in addition to technical skill and tactical preparation, includes mental rehearsal where the player plays the forthcoming match in their head. They will visualize themselves playing at their best, reading their opponent easily, spotting openings and attacking their opponent's weaknesses with themselves in a space of calm assertiveness, moving with ease and winning rallies. This process of mental rehearsal is repeated intermittently over the build up period right through to the final warm-up, which will prepare the body and spirit to compete.

Four Hours Prior
Eat a light carbohydrate meal or a couple of bananas, staying well relaxed with a little mental rehearsal.

Two Hours Prior
Try to be relaxed and keep sipping fluids. Carbohydrate drinks will be of great benefit at this stage and maybe a cereal bar to make certain that your carbohydrate level is topped up.

One Hour Prior
Remember that a warm-up will prepare the body and mind to compete, with everything working at a pace that it will need to work at as soon as the words 'love all' are heard! To start the warm-up do some steady walking, building up to jogging, followed by some easy stretching for all the joints and muscle groups. Next, go back to the light jogging, but this time build up to some short bursts of running at approximately half pace.

If you can find a free court – great! Start with some rhythm-based driving to length, building to some angle play. Position yourself just in front of the T-zone, striking alternate backhand and forehand so that the ball hits the front wall, then the sidewall, coming back to you in the T-zone. Build this pace gradually until you are striking at maximum pace, which will make the brain, as well as the body, work at maximum speed. Maintain this for at least 5min. If no court is available, find some space and simulate the process with some ghosting.

Working Roles and Relationships in Squash

There are a number of relationships in squash that can significantly affect the performance and attitude of the player: firstly, the player's personal relationships with parents or guardians and, if they have one, their partner; secondly, the player's relationship with other members of their team and other players; thirdly, the relationship between the player and their coach, which is perhaps the most important. This latter relationship can be an emotional roller-coaster and consists of a delicate balance between advice, instruction, cajoling, argument, support, friendship and acceptance.

What advice can this book give with regard to the three above relationships? The most important thing is to appreciate the role, influence and responsibility that each has for the other. The most effective way to do this is to ensure that there is regular communication and discussion between all the parties at the appropriate level. Below I outline what are considered to be the essential elements of each of these relationships.

The Coach

It is the coach's role to develop the player and the player's role to make the most of that opportunity. How they go about this is the key to whether a partnership is a success or not. The values and goals of both the player and the coach need to be closely aligned in order for the two of them to work together towards a common aim rather than at cross purposes. It will come as no surprise when I say I believe that mutual respect, trust and integrity are at the heart of any success. It is important that both the player and the coach mature and grow together. Some of the most successful relationships are where the player and coach continually nudge each other to get better and each responds to that challenge in a positive manner. The more experienced players are able to accurately predict what is

Hard at work. Tough decisions require consultation from the refs and markers.

disappointed in them not in how a decision or a game went. As a coach you have to be particularly careful how you express yourself and how you appear to the child in order to communicate your message accurately. Young children are less able to take criticism in a positive way so it is even more important to stress the positives in their game and, over time, gently correct the negatives.

Coaches (and parents) should avoid the temptation to interfere and correct errors too often. One of the most important abilities a young player can develop is good decision-making, so it is sensible to allow the player as much freedom as possible to make their own decisions and correct their own mistakes. Obviously you will need to step in if a decision is inappropriate or unsafe.

Parents

With younger players, parents are an important factor. It is often the parents that the coach has most difficulty with. Parents are naturally protective towards their children and are often unable or unwilling to view their child in the same way as the coach. They may have unrealistically high expectations of the potential of their child and expect the coach to devote their time developing that potential. It can be hard to accept that your child is not in an elite group, but remember that trying to push your child forward and forcing them to compete at too high a level will likely put them off playing squash for a long time. Both parents and coaches should bear in mind that talent identification in young children is extraordinarily difficult, and while a child may seem much better than their peers this is not a reliable indicator of long-term development and future success.

Coaches should also bear in mind that the parents have probably made many sacrifices to get their child to competitions and training and can get frustrated when they believe their efforts are not being rewarded. Communication here is essential: 'what do the parents have in mind for their child and how does it differ from

about to happen in a game and respond appropriately. This process, commonly described as read–decision–action, needs to be developed through appropriate coaching, practice, training, competition and feedback. Too often, coaching has overemphasized technique – action – over reading and decision-making skills. The coach should provide the player with equal opportunities to develop his perception and decision-making skills. Reading skills can be developed by exposing the player to non-identical but similar situations so that they understand and interpret the differences, whereas decision-making can be developed by providing a safe learning environment where players can experiment and try out things for themselves, and get feedback on the results.

Young Players

It has been said many times, and it is worth repeating, 'children are not small adults'. They are not capable of the same decisions that adults make because their brains are simply not wired that way during their formative years. They have much shorter attention spans and can have difficulty remembering a list of instructions. The ability to process information quickly and sift out the irrelevant detail is also less developed and, as a consequence, they are not as quick to make decisions. It can be harder for a child to make sacrifices now, in the present, in anticipation of future success and, as a result, they can find it more difficult to engage in training at the expense of playing. Obviously the coach needs to introduce good skills through practice but also needs to ensure frequent interludes of fun.

How a coach communicates with a young player can make or break the relationship with them. To a child the world can appear in black and white, whereas adults are able to introduce shades of grey. If a child sees that you are disappointed they are likely to assume that you are

Some young volunteers with their coach and mentor.

practices on court, can help during this period.

As players go through puberty their brains rewire themselves in order to become adult, but this process may not complete itself until the late teens. As this process progresses, teenagers can become sulky, irrational and argumentative. They become less cautious in the way they behave, which could lead them to act before they think. This can be a particular issue in boys because, combined with a boost in testosterone, it can cause them to become more aggressive. Fortunately it has been shown that involvement in squash, as well as other physical sports, can give much-needed release for this aggression. At this stage it is a good idea to involve the player in more of the decision-making about training and also in the general training process. This will help them feel that your relationship with them is moving to a more adult level. As teenagers, their social group also takes on greater importance and, while there may be little you can do about this, you do need to appreciate that their priorities in life may be changing. Once again, good communication is vital and allows the player to discuss their priorities and ensure their continued involvement in the game.

The Player

It is important that the player's actions and behaviour help the coaching process. This involves things that are largely within the player's control. Make sure you are where you are supposed to be at the correct time, it is frustrating for a coach if a player turns up late to training or competition. The coach will be distracted from doing what is important by worrying about whether you're going to turn up or not. It is also the player's responsibility to turn up with the right equipment and any additional extras such as drinks or food. Perhaps most important is that you turn up with the right attitude. There is nothing more frustrating to a coach than a player with genuine talent who refuses to apply himself fully.

what the coach has in mind?' If the parents and coach don't agree on this, it will lead to conflict. Ultimately, it is the coach's responsibility to train the player and the coach should be happy that the training regime is suitable for the player and will produce the best results.

The Maturing Player

As the player matures, there will be many changes. Physical maturity brings mostly

positives in squash, but the process of maturing can cause difficulties for the player. We are all familiar with gangly teenagers who seem unable to control their arms and legs. This is because as the body grows, and particularly if it grows quickly, the brain has to readjust to where everything is. The proprioceptive system, which gives the body its awareness of each of its parts, can take time to adjust, so players are likely to suffer a dip in form during this process. Exercises that improve coordination, as well as rhythm-based

As a younger player be careful that you
are not pulled in different directions by
your coach and your parents. Your coach
should tend to your development as a
player; your parents should tend to your
development as a person. This is not to
say that your coach does not care about
other aspects of your life, but their special-
ism is squash. Your parents will guide you
in all aspects of your life. An example of
this would be a tournament taking place
in the middle of your exams. There may
be conflict over your commitment to
the tournament and your commitment
to revise. Again, good communication is
essential. Your coach may not be aware
of how important the exams are to your
future, or your parents may not know
how important the tournament is to your
squash development.

As a young player your coach and
parents will guide you, but as you grow
older you will be in a position to assert
your own authority. At this stage the
relationship between you and your coach
and you and your parents will need to
change. As you grow older and gain more
independence you will also become more
responsible for yourself. You may also have
a clearer idea of how you wish to develop
as a player and as a person. You will need
to weigh up your priorities in squash and
in life. Teenagers face some difficult decisions at this time – socializing with friends
takes on greater importance, there are
exams to consider which will affect their

Enjoy the competition. It's got to be good for you.

future, they have choices to make on their
future education, they seek some financial
independence and so may look for a part-
time job – all of these aspects have to be
weighed against their future in squash. In
the end, the player has to make his own
choice about where to spend his time and
effort, and some rational discussion with
his parents and coaches will help him make
the right decision.

The Brain Game

What Makes a Winner?

At any stage you have a choice over what
you want to do. *You* have chosen to play
squash or participate in a business or
education programme etc. The aim here
is to help you find out exactly how your
choice was made and the reasons for it,
that is, your motivation for taking part. This
is important because sometimes it may not
feel that it was your choice – pressures
put on you from outside, such as parents,

coaches, teachers, friends etc. may have
influenced you choice – but remember
that you can always say 'no', even though
it may seem difficult or even impossible at
the time. Keep reading and you will gain
the confidence to make the decision for
yourself. In order to succeed *you* need to
make the choice that you are going to fully
commit to this programme. You cannot
sit back and wait for the world to come
to you or moan that no one understands
your true potential and that is why you
never succeed.

It is important to do your very best at
what you want to try; only then will you
know your own abilities and potential
and make your choice based on facts and
dreams. Knowledge is one thing, applying
it is another. You can finish up as knowl-
edgeable as any squash player or coach
in the world, but if you do not apply that
knowledge when you play it will be of no
help at all.

Remember also that knowledge,
understanding and application are different
elements and are generally achieved over

a period of time. It is a process, not an instant transformation. You must practise in order to improve. For some, improvement may be quick, for others it will be slower. However, as long as you are applying yourself, the speed of improvement is not important. The journey to success will not be a straight line – often it will involve leaps forward – and you must expect to stall occasionally or you will slip back and have to start again. This is *normal* and you will need to identify sources of support to help you through these times.

What Stops You Being Your Best?

We are motivated by pleasure and pain – we seek pleasure and avoid pain. Since failure brings hurt, it often dominates our thoughts more than the possibility of success, and many people are motivated to avoid failure rather than seek success for its own sake. The better we become as players, the more others expect us to succeed. This brings greater pressure as the perceived reward for success lessens (it is expected – the norm; it is no longer seen as such a big achievement). On the other hand, because success is expected, by definition failure is unexpected, so the penalty for failure is perceived to be even greater than before. This can lead to a vicious circle – the better you get the more you have to fear from failure and the less recognition you get from success.

We all have our own beliefs, and some are irrefutable, such as 'I am a human being.' Some can be rationalized: 'I believe global warming is a problem.' Some are not so rational: 'I am not allowed to fail.' It is important to keep things in perspective.

What Do You Need to Do to Improve?

Two things are essential: firstly, and most importantly, *you* must want to improve; secondly, identify what you need to work on to make the biggest difference. This is important because if you work hard at the wrong things you won't see the improve-

ment you want and you may start to lose motivation.

Imagine that you are going to act as a scout for someone you are coaching. You will watch their next opponent and identify their critical weaknesses. You are then going to coach your player to beat that opponent by exploiting their top five weaknesses to the full. Why the top five? Because any more than five would be difficult to coach and difficult to remember.

What if the player you were checking out were you? What weaknesses would you identify? What aspects would you coach yourself to exploit? You now have a list of five things to work on. If you concentrate on these you will become a better player. Improving on these five weaknesses will substantially enhance your ability and bring you closer to being the success you want to be.

Which one should you start with? Always start with the weakness you least want to work on, which is likely to be the one that is most difficult and the one that will play most on your mind. Resolve that weakness and the rest will follow.

What Happens if I Fail?

Everybody fails at some time or another. There isn't anyone in the world that succeeded with an 11–0, 11–0, 11–0 win first time they stepped on to the court. If you come across someone who tells you that they did succeed first time at everything, tell them that they just failed to impress you!

There are only two reasons why you may fail:

1   You are not good enough at the moment – learn from your experience and go back and work on your top five areas for improvement. At some stage, of course, you may have to face up to the fact that you never will be good enough. In which case, rejoice, and turn your attention to enjoying squash at this level for the rest of your life.
2   You didn't prepare properly.

The first reason is easy to deal with: be mature, go away and improve, learn more about whatever is necessary to become a better player. The second is more difficult to explain. Why did you fail to prepare properly for something that you said you wanted? You may need better advice, more coaching or more practice.

Help

Ask for help as soon as you realize you need it. People often wait until they have no alternative but to get help. If you wait this long you will be in more trouble and it will be more difficult to improve. It may come as a surprise, but others often don't realize that you need or want help and the only way they will help is through a direct request: 'I am struggling with … Can you help me?' If you casually refer to the fact that some help would be nice or others always seem to get more help than you, they might just agree and leave you to it.

You cannot be serious? An appeal to the referee.

Human beings are *not* mind-readers; *ask* directly (and politely of course).

Do remember to follow up and chase your help. Are they coming when they say so? Check exactly what they can do for you. Check and double-check everything. If you assume and get it wrong, everyone's time has been wasted. This may sound paranoid or pessimistic but it is not. Expecting the worst is being pessimistic; preparing to overcome the worst is prudent and is how to achieve success. There is a phrase 'the meaning of a communication is the response it gets'. This means that regardless of what you thought you said or did to someone else, it is how they interpret it that will matter to you. So get them to check back with you to confirm they understood what you meant.

Motivation

The issue of motivation is one that is highly important to players and coaches alike. How is it that despite setting goals and a training strategy with their coach, a player can still lack the commitment to train or, worse still, to compete?

Some people interpret motivation as simply psyching yourself up for the big game, but motivation is far more complex. Both players and coaches have their reasons for taking part in squash, and these reasons are subject to change over time. A player may begin to play squash simply because his friends do; over time, as they improve, they may enjoy the challenge of competition; later in life they may see it as a means of staying fit. Whatever a player's reasons for participating, it is important for both the coach and the player to understand the sources of their motivation.

Very simply, motivation can be divided into two areas:

- self-motivation (intrinsic) where the player looks to improve and compete for the personal satisfaction of doing so
- external motivation (extrinsic) where the player seeks external rewards such as rankings, trophies and recognition.

Once the reasons for a player taking part in squash are established, and they are likely to be a combination of the above, both the coach and the player can use these reasons to motivate themselves. The driving force behind motivation is what the person wants in the end; in other words their goals. It is the coach's job to acquaint themselves with these goals and tailor the training and competition in order to help the player achieve them.

When a coach is using extrinsic rewards in order to enhance motivation, he needs to consider the following:

- how often they are used
- when they are used

RIGHT: *It can be tough at the top.*

BELOW: *A good contest.*

S	• Specific – state exactly what you want in positive terms
M	• Measurable – so you can assess your progress • Meaningful – so it has importance to you
A	• Accepted – agreed by both the coach and the player • As if – you can imagine yourself 'as if' you are already there
R	• Realistic – it is something you can achieve • Resources – you have the necessary resources or can find them
T	• Timed – provide a specific time frame for achieving the goal
E	• Exciting – it creates enthusiasm in the player and the coach • Ecological – it doesn't adversely affect other areas of your life such as friends, family, school, work, etc.
R	• Recorded – write down the goal and formally record your efforts and progress towards it • Recruit others to help you

Goal setting criteria.

- how quickly after a good performance they are used
- what the most effective reward would be
- the danger of a player becoming motivated only through extrinsic reward.

There are also tactics to enhance intrinsic motivation, such as:

- manipulation of the environment to provide a successful experience
- rewards in line with the performance
- plenty of appropriate praise
- involving the player in the decision-making process
- setting realistic but challenging goals that are based on the player's ability.

In order to accurately assess the player's needs it is helpful to both the player and the coach to write down their goals. An acronym that is commonly used is

SMARTER, a version of which is described in the diagram above.

Specific – By stating exactly what you wish to achieve you allow everyone around you to offer appropriate help. Consider this if you want to improve your ranking by ten places but have just told your coach you want to get better. Your coach is likely to suggest a few things you could do to improve rather than design a targeted training programme. The goal needs to be stated in the positive, in other words 'this is what I want' – not 'this is what I don't want'.

Measurable – Allows you to test and review your performance to ensure that you are making the progress needed. If you can't compare where you have got to with where you have come from, it is difficult for anyone to assess whether you've made any improvement. By measuring your progress you can also double-check that you are on target to reach your goal or whether you need to reassess the goal or the training programme.

Meaningful – Something you feel for yourself. We can all set goals for ourselves but unless they have any value it is highly unlikely that we will succeed.

Accepted – It is important that both you and your coach agree on what you want to achieve since both of you are going to commit time and effort to the arrangement.

As if – You are unlikely to achieve your goal if you cannot imagine yourself as if you have achieved it.

Realistic – Goals should be optimistic and should be designed to push you, but any goal that pushes you too hard will have a demotivating effect.

Resources – Are you in a position to achieve this goal by yourself or are you going to need help and additional resources? Since you are going to need court time, coaching and equipment, have you checked that these things will be available to you?

xciting – If the goal doesn't excite you, hen you need to question your motiva- on to achieve it.

cological – Does this goal suit your eeds not just as a player but also as a erson? If, in order to achieve your goal, ou have to give up something else that important to you such as friends, family, ork or education, you may find yourself conflict.

ecorded – Write down all the elements f your goal. This will fix what you need o do firmly in your mind and give you omething to refer back to in order to eep you on track.

ecruit – Tell others what your goals are. hey may be able to offer assistance and upport. Once you have told others what ou intend to do, it adds an additional ncentive to make sure you succeed. There re two types of goal: outcome goals hich set a defined outcome at the end f the process, for example 'I am going o win a gold medal next year at the European Championships', or performance goals which focus on a player's specific improvement in a specified area of the game that they have sole control over, for example 'I will ensure that 90 per cent of my serves land within six inches of the back of the court.'

It is best to strike an appropriate balance between the two types of goal. Outcome goals rely on the performance of other people as well as the player, so not all the factors are within the player's control. It is a good idea to set an outcome goal that is supported by a number of performance goals.

By the time you have finished this comprehensive process you will have a full understanding of your goal and exactly what you need to do to achieve it. It will also highlight any areas where you are unsure and so give you the opportunity to review and explore those elements in detail. Be prepared to go through the process more than once in order to get it exactly right for you. There is no harm in re-drafting your goals as long as you are not looking for an excuse to avoid starting.

> **TOP TIPS**
>
> - Use a number of performance goals to support a single outcome goal
> - Create a series of short-term goals to enable you to reach a longer-term goal; by doing this you give yourself a series of mini successes on the way to greater success
> - Ensure that you do something daily to take yourself closer to the goal, whether this is practice, a game, fitness training, watching a role model, or simply reading a book about squash
> - Ask for help as soon as you realize you need it
> - Treat failure as a learning experience and do better next time
> - Start now!

me to push hard.

SUMMARY OF WINNERS

World Open/World Individual

Geoff Hunt (Aus): 1967* 1969* 1971*
1976 1979 1980
Cam Nancarrow (Aus): 1973*
Kevin Shawcross (Aus): 1976*
Maqsood Ahmed (Pak): 1977*
Jahangir Khan (Pak): 1979* 1981 1982
   1983 1983* 1984 1985 1988
Steve Bowditch (Aus): 1981*
Ross Norman (Nzl): 1986
Jansher Khan (Pak): 1987 1989 1990 1992
1993 1994 1995 1996
Rodney Martin (Aus): 1991
Rodney Eyles (Aus): 1997
Jonathon Power (Can): 1998
Peter Nicol (Sco): 1999
David Palmer (Aus): 2002 2006
Amr Shabana (Egy): 2003 2005 2007 2009
Thierry Lincou (Fra): 2004
Ramy Ashour (Egy): 2008
Nick |Matthew (Eng): 2010

*World Amateur/Individual

World Men's Team

Australia 1967 1969 1971 1973 1989
   1991 2001 2003
Great Britain 1976 1979
Pakistan 1977 1981 1983 1985 1987 1993
England 1995 1997 2005 2007
Egypt 1999 2009

World Women's Open

Heather McKay (Aus) 1979
Rhonda Thorne (Aus) 1981
Vicki Cardwell (Aus) 1983
Susan Devoy (Nzl) 1985 1987 1990 1992
Martine le Moignan (Eng) 1989
Michelle Martin (Aus) 1993 1994 1995
Sarah Fitz-Gerald (Aus) 1996 1997 1998
   2001 2002
Cassie Campion (née Jackman) (Eng) 1999
Carol Owens (Aus/Nzl) 2000 2003
Vanessa Atkinson (Ned) 2004
Nicol David (Mas) 2005 2006 2008 2009
Rachael Grinham (Aus) 2007

World Women's Team

Great Britain 1979
Australia 1981 1983 1992 1994 1996
   1998 2002 2004 2010
England 1985 1987 1989 1990 2000 2006
Egypt 2008

CODE OF CONDUCT FOR SQUASH COACHES

Introduction

Coaches play a critical role in the personal and physical development of the people they coach. Squash coaches shall therefore adhere at all times to standards of personal behaviour which reflect credit on England Squash, Scottish Squash, Squash Wales, Ulster Squash and the whole process, practice and profession of coaching.

This code of conduct has been developed to clarify and determine approved and accepted professional, ethical and moral behaviour.

Squash coaches have a responsibility to:

- ensure the health and safety of all players with whom they work
- provide a safe environment that maximizes benefits and minimizes risks to players in achieving their goals
- create an environment in which individuals are motivated to maintain participation and improve performance
- treat all players equally, regardless of gender, ability, place of origin, colour, sexual orientation, religion, political belief or economic status
- ensure that the activities being coached are suitable for the age, maturity, experience, ability and fitness level of the players
- know and understand the rules of squash and coach players to play within the rules and spirit of the game at all times
- be a positive role model and act as an ambassador for the sport of squash

- consistently display high personal standards and professional behaviour
- refrain from public criticism of fellow coaches
- regularly seek ways of increasing professional development and self-awareness and become a licensed coach
- recognize and accept when to refer players to other coaches and sport specialists
- place the needs and interests of the player before their own and before the development of performance
- foster a culture of loyalty, openness, trust, mutual respect, honesty and encourage and guide players to accept responsibility for their own behaviour and performance
- promote the concept of a balanced lifestyle, supporting the well-being of the player both in and out of the sport of squash.

Coaches must:

- not engage in behaviour that constitutes any form of abuse (physical, sexual, emotional, neglect, bullying)
- develop an appropriate working relationship with players (especially children), based on mutual trust and respect
- coaches must not exert undue influence to obtain personal benefit or reward
- avoid sexual intimacy with players
- take appropriate action regarding concerns about the behaviour of an adult towards a child

- maintain confidentiality when appropriate and avoid situations that would potentially create a conflict of interest or exploit the player
- at the outset, clarify with players (and where appropriate with their parents) exactly what is expected of them and what players are entitled to expect from their coach (including detailing any video or photography work which may be undertaken as a coaching tool)
- not solicit business away from any other coaches or clubs
- not misrepresent their qualification, affiliations, or professional competence to any client or prospective client in any publication, broadcast, lecture, seminar or displayed advertising
- only undertake coaching which is within the parameters of their coaching awards/qualifications
- have appropriate public liability insurance
- have completed a Personal Disclosure Form and returned it to England Squash/Squash Wales or a Disclosure Scotland Form and returned it to Scottish Squash
- possess a current and valid Criminal Records Bureau Enhanced Disclosure (not required in Scotland)
- report all criminal convictions in a court of law to the National Squash Governing Body at the earliest opportunity
- support the National Squash Governing Body in the development of squash.

Complaints Procedures/ Personal Misconduct

Personal misconduct by squash coaches may give rise to disciplinary action by the National Squash Governing Body. Any individual or organization wishing to make a complaint against a squash coach within the context of this Code of Conduct should in the first instance contact the National Squash Governing Body's Chief Executive (England, Wales) Chief Operating Officer (Scotland), or Director of Performance and Education (Ulster).

Disciplinary Procedure

The exact nature of the offence will determine the appropriate course of action in any particular situation. All coaches will be treated impartially and no acts of favouritism or discrimination will be permitted.

*   A squash coach will render himself/ herself liable to disciplinary action if the Code of Conduct for Squash Coaches is breached.
*   The coach will be informed of the nature of the breach as laid against him/her as soon as possible and will have the opportunity and the right to state their case before any decision regarding the appropriate disciplinary action is taken.
*   When the facts have been established and responsibility is clear, disciplinary action can consist of any of the following:
    *   verbal warning
    *   written warning
    *   Coach's Licence being revoked.

As part of my membership to the Coach Licence Scheme I agree to abide by all of the above principles.

There's always a chance!

GLOSSARY

Aerobic   The production of energy in the presence of oxygen.
Anaerobic   The production of energy without oxygen.

Carbohydrate   A food made up of sugars and/or starches which provides the body with energy.
Core stability   The middle part of the body is in balance.

Dehydration   A decrease in the body's stores of fluid.

Energy   Is derived from the breakdown of foodstuffs and is used to provide the body with the capacity to exercise.

Fat   Is a food composed of fatty acid and glycerol which provides the body with energy.
Fitness   Is a term used to describe the physical condition of the body.
Flexibility   The range of movement in a joint.

Ghosting   The repetition of squash-specific movement(s) without a ball or an opponent.

Interval running   A form of running with high intensity interspersed with rest and/or periods of light running.

Isotonic drinks   Drinks with the same dissolved particles as body fluid.

Kill   To strike the ball so that it is non-returnable.

Lactic acid   An end-product of anaerobic breakdown of glucose or glycogen.
Let   To replay a rally.
Lob   To strike the ball with great height and without pace.

Macro-cycle   A long-term training programme.
Meso-cycle   A two-month phase of an overall training programme focused on a specific component of fitness.
Micro-cycle   A small block of training sessions over two weeks.

Nick   The join of the floor and wall of the court.

Overload   A progressive increase in the amount of work the body is required to do for improvement.
Overtraining   A state of exhaustion brought about by excessive exercise.

Periodization   Identification of specific phases in a competitive and training year.
Plyometric exercises   Where muscles are rapidly pre-stretched before being contracted.

Protein   Food made up of amino acids, which provides the body with the function of muscle growth, repair and energy.

Racket   An implement with which to strike the ball.
Racquets   An early version of the game of squash.
Rally   A series of strikes of the ball before a point is scored.
Respiration   The process of gas exchange in the lungs.

Speed   A measure of the distance a person can cover in a specific time.
Strength   The ability of muscles to exert force.

T-zone   The central part of the court.
Tactics   A method to achieve an outcome.
Tapering   A progressive reduction in the training load in preparation for competition.

Volley   To strike the ball before it has bounced.

Warm-up   To prepare the body both mentally and physically to compete or train.

You only get points if you go for them! Taking the chance even when you are off balance can pay dividends.

USEFUL CONTACTS AND ADDRESSES

World Squash Federation
8 Russell Street
Hastings
East Sussex TN34 1QU, England
Tel: 00 44 1424 447440
Fax: 00 44 1424 430737
Email: admin@worldsquash.org

Affiliates

PSA
Tour Director, Professional Squash Association
23 Cathedral Road
Cardiff CF11 9PH, Wales
Tel: (44) 2920 388446
Fax: (44) 2920 228185
Email: psa@psa-squash.com
www.psa-squash.com

WISPA
Administrator, WISPA
7 Westminster Palace Gardens
Artillery Row
London SW1P 1RR, England
Tel: (44) 207 222 1667
Fax: (44) 207 976 8778
Email: wispahq@aol.com
www.wispa.net

Arab
President, Arab Squash Federation
C/o Egyptian Squash Federation
07 El Tayran Street
Nasr City
Cairo, Egypt
Tel: (20) 225 780 234/(20) 224 010 23
Fax: (20) 227 703 150

CASA
President, Caribbean Area Squash Association (CASA)
C/o Barbados Squash Rackets Association
Barbados Olympic Association Inc
PO Box 387

Olympic Centre
Garfield Sobers Sports Complex
Wildey
St Michael, BB 15094, Barbados
www.caribbeansquash.org

EASF
President, East Asian Squash Federation (EASF)
c/o Korea Squash Federation
503 Olympic Hall
88 Oryun-Dong
Songpa-Gu
Seoul, Korea, 138-749

WDSI
Technical Director, World Deaf Squash Inc.
20 Flamboro Close
Eastwood
Leigh on Sea
Essex SS9 5NT, England
Tel: 01702 512781
Email: worlddeafsquash@sky.com
www.worlddeafsquash.com

Regional Federations

Africa
Secretary General, Squash Federation of Africa
PO Box 613
Northlands
2116 Gauteng, South Africa
Tel: (27) 11 442 8056
Fax: (27) 11 442 8036

Asia
Secretary General, Asian Squash Federation
Pusat Skuasy Nasional
Kompleks Sukan Negara
Bukit Jalil, Sri Petaling
57000 Kuala Lumpur, Malaysia
Tel: (603) 8996 3964

Fax: (603) 8996 9406
Email: asiasquash@gmail.com
www.asiansquash.com

European Squash Federation
The Almonry
High Street
Battle
East Sussex TN33 0EA, England
Tel: +44 1424 774058
Registered No: 04628339

Member Nations

Austria
(Founded 1978)
President: Michael Khan
Secretary: Andy Holland
Secretariat: Osterreichischer Squash Rackets Verband, c/o Danube Freizeitanlagen GmbH, Franzosengraben 2, 1030 Vienna, Austria
Tel: +43 660 481 5948
Fax: +43 660 33 481 5948
Email: office@squash.or.at
www.squash.or.at
Clubs/Courts: 57/450

Belgium
(Founded 1974)
President: Stéphane Ibourki
Secretary: Ann van de Wouwer
Secretariat: Belgian Squash Federation, Vorselaarsebaan 64, 2200 Herentals, Belgium
Tel: +32 14 85 9604
Fax: +32 14 36 8855
Email: vsf@vsf.be
www.squash.be

Secretariat: Flemish Squash Federation, Vorselaarsebaan 64, 2200 Herentals, Belgium
Secretary: Ann van de Wouwer
Tel: +32 14 85 9600

Fax: +32 14 36 8855
Email: vsf@vsf.be
www.vsf.be

Secretariat: Ligue Francophone de Squash
ASBL, Chaussée de Wavre 2057 (Boîte
R14), Auderghem, 1160 Brussels, Belgium
Director: Laurent Bensalah
Tel: +32 473 42 08 39
Fax: +32 2 410 22 51
Email: info.lfs@squash.be
www.lfs.be
Clubs/Courts: 107/507

Croatia
(Founded 2001)
President: Vedran Rezic
Secretary: Davor Srednoselec
Secretariat: Croatian Squash Federation,
Stubička 52, 10 000 Zagreb, Croatia
Tel: +385 1 3697 299/+385 98 218 166
(V Rezic)/+385 99 619 6667
(D Srednoselec)
Fax: +385 1 6114 518
Email: vedran.rezic@squashtower.hr/
davor@squashtower.hr
www.cro-squash.hr
Clubs/Courts: 5/12

Cyprus
(Founded 1983)
President: Michael G Hadjikyriacos
Secretary: Nicholas Christofides
Email: n.christofides@frederick.ac.cy
Secretariat: Cyprus Squash Rackets Federa-
tion, PO Box 27109, 1642 Nicosia, Cyprus
Tel: +357 2283 2131
Fax: +357 2283 3892
Email: squashcy@cytanet.com.cy
www.cytanet.com.cy/squashcy
Clubs/Courts: 7/30

Czech Republic
(Founded 1992)
Chairman: Miroslav Valenta
Secretary: Filip Vladyka
Secretariat: Czech Squash Association
(CASQ), Zátopkova 10/2, 160 17 Praha 6,
Strahov, Czech Republic
Tel: +420 777 638 360
Fax: +420 242 429 243
Email: casq@casq.cz
www.casq.cz
Clubs/Courts: 49/278

Denmark
(Founded 1971)
President: Tom Kjaerbye Larsen
Secretary: Carsten Lausten
Secretariat: Dansk Squash Forbund,
Stadionvej 47 st tv, 5200 Odense V,
Denmark
Tel: +45 66 190 822
Fax: +45 66 130 198
Email: squash@dsqf.dk/carsten@dsqf.dk
www.dsqf.dk
Clubs/Courts: 55/203

England
(Founded 1928)
President: Jackie Robinson OBE
Chief Executive Officer: Nick Rider
Secretariat: England Squash and Racket-
ball National Squash Centre, Sportcity,
Rowsley Street, Manchester M11 3FF,
England
Tel: +44 161 231 4499
Fax: +44 161 231 4231
Email: enquiries@englandsquashandracket-
ball.com
www.englandsquashandracketball.com
Clubs/Courts: 1200/2419

Estonia
(Founded 1997)
President: Henn Ruubel
Chairman: Zoran Grojic
Secretariat: Estonian Squash Federation,
Väike-Ameerika 19, Tallinn 10129, Estonia
Tel: +372 501 3747
Fax: +372 627 0769
Email: zoran@squash.ee
www.squash.ee
Clubs/Courts: 15/25

Finland
(Founded 1971)
President: Leo Hatjasalo
Executive Director: Hannu Mäkinen
Email: hannu.makinen@squash.fi
Secretary: Satu Kiipeli
Secretariat: Suomen Squashlitto, Radiokatu
20, 00093 SLU, Helsinki, Finland
Tel: +358 9 3481 2400
Fax: +358 9 3481 2411
Email: squash.office@squash.fi
www.squash.fi
Clubs/Courts: 55/315

France
(Founded 1981)
President: Jacques Fontaine
Secretary General: Frédérique Roualen
National Technical Director: Jacques Lagrange
Secretariat: Fédération Française de
Squash, 2 rue de Paris, 94100 St Maur des
Fossés, France
Tel: +33 1 5512 3490
Fax: +33 1 5512 3491
Email: contact@ffsquash.com
www.ffsquash.com
Clubs/Courts: 385/801

Germany
(Founded 1973)
President: Wolfgang Bauriedel
Email: wolfgang.bauriedel@gmx.de
Secretary: Beate Leuchtenberg
Secretariat: Deutscher Squash Verband eV
(DSQV), Amselweg 10, 46395 Bocholt,
Germany
Tel: +49 251 975 6335
Fax: +49 251 890 5625
Email: office@dsqv.de
http://dsqv.de
Clubs/Courts: 500/6000

Gibraltar
(Founded 1961)
President: Barry Brindle
Secretary: Victor Camilleri
Secretariat: Gibraltar Squash Association,
PO Box 729, Gibraltar
Tel: +350 44922
Fax: +350 72228
Email: info@gibsquash.com
www.gibsquash.com
Clubs/Courts: 1/4

Greece
(Founded 1974)
President: George Barletis
Secretary: Marc Passaliadis
Secretariat: Greek Squash Rackets
Federation, Kronou 19, P Faliro,
17564 Athens, Greece
Tel: +30 210 982 0645/+30 210 961
6967/+30 210 895 8428
Fax: +30 210 924 3629
Email: marc1@hol.gr
Vice-President: Mohamed Samanoudi
Email: saman@ath.forthnet.gr
Clubs/Courts: 9/20

Hungary
(Founded 1989)
President: István Szöcs
Email: iszocs@squash.hu
Secretary: Gabor Képes
Secretariat: Magyar Fallabda (Squash)
Szövetség, c/o Lite Wellness Klub,
Csorsz u 14-16, 1123 Budapest,
Hungary
Tel: +36 20 9511 117
Fax: +36 1 310 7348
Email: gkepes@squash.hu
www.squash.hu
Clubs/Courts: 16/34

Iceland
(Founded 1988)
President: Tomas Gudbjartsson
Chairman: Hilmar H. Gunnarsson
Secretary: Valdimar Oskarsson
Secretariat: Iceland Squash, Stórhöfdi 17,
110 Reykjavik, Iceland
Tel: +354 577 5555
Fax: +354 577 5577
Email: veggsport@veggsport.is
www.veggsport.is
Clubs/Courts: 6/10

Ireland
(Founded 1935)
President: John O'Connor
Operations Manager: Cathy Quinn
Secretariat: Irish Squash, Sport HQ,
13 Joyce Way, Park West, Dublin 12,
Ireland
Tel: +353 1 625 1145
Fax: +353 1 625 1146
Email: info@irishsquash.com
www.irishsquash.com
Clubs/Courts: 93/205

Isle of Man
(Founded 1988)
President: Leslie Callow
Chairman: Richard Corlett
Secretary: Ashley Sandyford-Sykes
Secretariat: Isle of Man Squash Rackets
Association, Ballavarvane House, St Marks,
Isle of Man, IM9 3AH
Tel: +44 7624 270003
Email: ashley.sandyfordsykes@googlemail.
com
www.iomsra.com
Clubs/Courts: 3/16

Israel
(Founded 1982)
Chairman: Dr Reuven Metrany
Office Manager: Amir Stern
ESF contact: Moshe Avraham
Secretariat: Israel Squash Rackets Associa-
tion, 27 Yaara St, Raanana 43220, Israel
Tel: +972 9 742 3583
Fax: +972 9 741 2225
Email: squashisrael@gmail.com
www.squashisrael.org
Clubs/Courts: 10/32

Italy
(Founded 1976)
President: Siro Zanella
Secretary: Davide Monti
Secretariat: Federazione Italiana Giuoco
Squash, Viale Forlimpopoli no 5, 47838
Riccione (RN), Italy
Tel: +390 541 790 894
Fax: +390 541 790 994
Email: info@federsquash.it
www.figs.it
Clubs/Courts: 340/492

Latvia
(Founded 2002)
President: Alex Pavulans
Secretariat: Latvian Squash Federation,
Stirnu iela 10, Rīga, LV-1082, Latvia
Tel: +371 2828 5930
Email: alex@institute.lv
www.squash.lv
Clubs/Courts: 4/15

Liechtenstein
(Founded 1988)
President: Oliver Stahl
Email: oliverstahl@powersurf.li
Vice-President: Gerhard Schober
Email: gerhard@schober.li
Secretariat: Liechtenstein Squash Rackets
Association, Fuerst Franz Josef Strasse 19,
FL-9490 Vaduz, Liechtenstein
Tel: +423 373 4833/+423 232 9686
Fax: +423 373 4841/+423 232 9692
Email: office@squash.li
www.squash.li
Clubs/Courts: 1/5

Luxembourg
(Founded 1973)
President: Georges Kieffer

Secretary/Treasurer: Adrian Roadway
Secretariat: Fédération Luxembourgeoise
de Squash Rackets, PO Box 1255, L-1012
Luxembourg
Tel: +352 264 88350
Fax: +352 264 88610
Email: GKieffer@luxconsult.lu
www.fsl.lu
Clubs/Courts: 10/25

Macedonia
President: Bojan Dukoski
Vice-President: Dr Vladimir Cadikovski
Secretary: Ivan Jovanovski
Secretariat: Squash Federation of
Macedonia, Lazar Licenoski 31/2, SRC Kale,
Skopje, Republic of Macedonia
Tel: +389 232 27077
Fax: +389 232 27077
Email: info@squash.com.mk

Malta
(Founded 1986)
Chairman: Liz Said
Secretary: Stephen Rizzo
Secretariat: Malta Squash, Casa Said,
Triq Raheb Kurradu, San Pawl Tat-Targa,
Naxxa, Malta
Tel: +356 21 411 678
Fax: +356 21 418 705
Email: info@maltasquash.com
www.maltasquash.com
Clubs/Courts: 6/15

Monaco
(Founded 1978)
President: Dr Bruno Fissore
Secretary: Patrick Rubino
Secretariat: Fédération Monegasque de
Squash Rackets, Stade Louis II, 7 Avenue
des Castelans, 98000 Monaco
Tel: +377 92 054 222
Fax: +377 92 056 242
Email: squash@squash.asso.mc
Clubs/Courts: 2/5

Montenegro
(Founded 2006)
President: Miso Pejkovic
Secretary: Mila Mugosa
Secretariat: Montenegrin Squash Associa-
tion, Put Radomira Ivanovica bb 81000,
Podgorica, Montenegro

Tel: +382 2065 8340
Fax: +381 2065 8340
Email: montenegro-squash@t-com.me

Netherlands
(Founded 1938)
Chairman: Frits de Leeuw
General Manager: Marcel Borst
Email: marcel@squashbond.nl
Technical Director: Marc Veldkamp
Email: marc@squashbond.nl
Secretariat: Squash Bond Nederland,
Postbus 711, 2700 AS, Zoetermeer,
The Netherlands
Tel: +31 79 361 5400
Fax: +31 79 361 5395
Email: info@squashbond.nl
www.squash.nl
Clubs/Courts: 380/1714

Norway
(Founded 1980)
President: Ida Sonju (Ms)
Email: idafsonju@hotmail.com
Tel:/Mobile: +47 22 49 5813/+47 913 84
619
General Secretary: Reidun Ribesen
Secretariat: Norges Squashforbund,
Idrettens Hus Rogaland, PO Box 3033,
4095 Stavanger, Norway
Tel: +47 90 14 13 14
Fax: +47 5173 7851
Email: Reidun.Ribesen@nif.idrett.no
www.squash.no
Clubs/Courts: 34/250

Poland
(Founded 1995)
Chairman: Janusz Plencler
Foreign Affairs: Tomasz Banasiak
Email: rabiot@me.com
Secretary: Natalia Barenska
Secretariat: Polska Federacja Squasha,
Leszno 8/1, 01-192 Warsaw, Poland
Email: rabiot@me.com
Tel: +48 501 701 341
Fax: +48 22 862 4019
Email: biuro@pfs.com.pl
www.pfs.com.pl
Clubs/Courts: 20/60

Portugal
(Founded 2005)
President: Bruno Dias

Email: bruno.dias@correio-electronico.net
Secretariat Federação Nacional de Squash,
Rua Antonio Candido Pinto, 34-8 Esq,
4715-400, Braga, Portugal
Tel: +351 919 312 312
Email: fns@correio-electronico.net
www.pt-squash.org

Russia
(Founded 1990)
President: Dr Vitaly Pascal
Chief Executive: Dr Vladimir Lifshits
Secretariat: Russian Squash Federation,
Basmany tupic 10/12–23, 105064 Moscow,
Russia
Tel: +7 499 265 2696
Fax: +7 499 265 2696
Email: vlifshits@mail.ru/rsf@front.ru
Clubs/Courts: 7/12

Scotland
(Founded 1936)
President: Ron Pearman
Chief Executive Officer: John Dunlop
Secretariat: Scottish Squash, Caledonia
House, South Gyle, Edinburgh EH12 9DQ,
Scotland
Tel: +44 131 625 4425
Fax: +44 131 317 7202
Email: info@scottishsquash.org
www.scottishsquash.org
Clubs/Courts: 275/600

Serbia
(Founded 2001)
President: Čedomir Vitorović
Vice-President: Ivan Djordevic
Secretariat: Serbian Squash Association,
Kneza Višeslava st 27, 11000 Belgrade,
Serbia
Tel: +381 11 305 5807/+381 64 6400
182
Fax: +381 11 305 5808
Email: office@squash.rs/ivansabv@gmail.
com
www.squash.co.yu
Clubs/Courts: 3/6

Slovakia
(Founded 1993)
President: Martin Manik
Email: president@squash.sk
Secretary: Jana Manikova

ESF contact: Martin Manik
Secretariat: Slovak Squash Association
(SSQA), Junácka 6, 832 80 Bratislava,
Slovakia
Tel: +421 9058 58223/+421 902 347 315
(Martin Manik)
Email: president@squash.sk/gs@squash.sk
www.squash.sk
Clubs/Courts: 18/60

Slovenia
(Founded 1992)
President: Goran Vučković
Secretary: Miha Černe
Secretariat: Slovenian Squash
Association (SQZS), Cesta na Brdo 109,
1000 Ljubljana, Slovenia
Tel: +386 59 020 204
Fax: +386 42 362 281
Email: miha@squash.si
www.squash.si
Clubs/Courts: 7/41

Spain
(Founded 1978)
President: Rogelio Chantada
Secretary General: Paloma Gonzalez
Ardevinez
Secretariat: Real Federación Española de
Squash, Polideportivo de Alcobendas,
Crta Barajas KM 1,400, 28100 Alcobendas,
Madrid, Spain
Tel: +34 91 658 7104
Fax: +34 91 663 9468
Email: RFES@infonegocio.com
www.rfesquash.es
Clubs/Courts: 69/150

Sweden
(Founded 1965)
President: Ulf Karlsson
General Secretary: Thomas Troedsson
Secretariat: Svenska Squashforbundet,
Bollspelsvägen 3, 216 25 Malmö, Sweden
Tel: +46 40 377 825 (T. Troedsson
mobile: +46 70 555 1969)
Fax: +46 4037 7827
Email: tt@squash.se
www.squash.se
Clubs/Courts: 60/400

Switzerland
(Founded 1974)
President: Stefan Grundmann

Technical Director: Michael Müller
Financial Officer: Robert Meyer
Secretariat: Schweiz Squash Verband,
Pihltalstrasse 63, 8135 Langnau am Albis,
Switzerland
Tel: +41 43 377 7003
Fax: +41 43 377 7007
Email: swiss@squash.ch
www.squash.ch
Clubs/Courts: 72/622

Turkey
(Founded 2003)
President: Enver Oral
Vice-President: Tunc Limasollu
Email: tunc@limasollunaci.com
Secretary: Songül Kara
Secretariat: Turkish Squash
c/o Turkish Developing Sports Federation,
General Directorate of Youth and Sport,
Ulus Ishani A-Blok No 1005-1008, Ulus,
Ankara, Turkey
Tel: +90 312 310 2143
Fax: +90 312 310 2142
Email: gosbf@hotmail.com

Ukraine
(Founded 2004)
President: Taras Olechko
ISF contact: Roman Dolynych
Secretariat: Ukrainian Squash Federation,
5 Strutinskogo St, Office 604, 800 Kiev,
Ukraine
Tel: +38 09 568 77 192
Fax: +38 44 285 1091
Email: usf@squash.org.ua
Clubs/Courts: 6/10

Wales
(Founded 1947)
President: Alan James

Chairman: Phil Brailey
Administrator: Sue Evans
Secretariat: Squash Wales,
Welsh Institute of Sport, Sophia Gardens,
Cardiff, CF11 9SW, Wales
Tel: +44 845 846 0027
Fax: +44 29 2023 2737
Email: squashwales@squashwales.co.uk
www.squashwales.co.uk
Clubs/Courts: 110/259

Oceania
President and Executive Director
Oceania Squash Federation
23 Kinsella Street
Belmont Heights, QLD 4153, Australia
Tel: [H] (61) 7 3390 6694
Email: oceaniasquash@optusnet.com.au
www.oceaniasquash.org

Panamerica
Secretary of the Federation of Panamerica
c/o Confederação Brasileira de Squash
Rua Pastor William Richard Schisler
Filho, 1200 – 88034-100, Florianópolis –
Santa Catarina, Brazil
Tel/Fax: (55) 48 3335 6044
Mobile: (55) 48 9983 0841/(55) 48 7811
1344
www.squashflash.com

Sub-Regional Federations

Arab
President, Arab Squash Federation
c/o Egyptian Squash Federation
Al Ahram Organisation
El Gallaa Street
Cairo, Egypt
Tel: (20) 225 780 234/(20) 224 010 237
Fax: (20) 227 703 150/(20) 222 624 273

Caribbean
President, Caribbean Area Squash
Association (CASA)
c/o Barbados Squash Rackets Association
Barbados Olympic Association Inc
PO Box 387
Olympic Centre
Garfield Sobers Sports Complex
Wildey
St Michael, BB 15094, Barbados
www.caribbeansquash.org

Central America
Vice-President, Confederacion
Centroamericana de Squash
Apartado Postal 181-C
Metro 15
Guatemala City, Guatemala
www.squashflash.com

South America
President, Confederacion Sudamericana
de Squash
360 Street, No. 1121
Ranelagh
Buenos Aires, Postal Code (1876),
Argentina
Tel: (54) 11 4258 8923
Fax: (54) 11 4258 8923
Email: residenciasudamericasquash@
hotmail.com
www.squashflash.com

BUCS
British Universities & Colleges Sport
(BUCS)
20–24 Kings Bench Street
London SE1 0QX, England
Tel: 020 7633 5080
Fax: 020 3268 2120
Email: info@bucs.org.uk

Great touch! Soft hands are essential for good touch.

INDEX

OTHER TITLES IN THE
CROWOOD SPORTS GUIDE SERIES

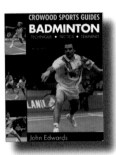

Badminton
JOHN EDWARDS

ISBN 978 1 86126 027 7

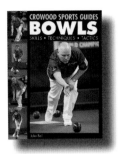

Bowls
JOHN BELL

ISBN 978 186126 968 3

Canoeing & Kayaking
MARCUS BAILLIE

ISBN 978 1 85223 528 4

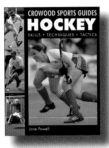

Hockey
JANE POWELL

ISBN 978 1 84797 122 7

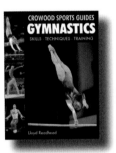

Gymnastics
LLOYD READHEAD

ISBN 978 1 84797 247 7

Netball
ANITA NAVIN

ISBN 978 1 84797 042 8

Orienteering
CAROL MCNEILL

ISBN 978 1 84797 206 4

Rugby Union
PETER JOHNSON

ISBN 978 1 84797 064 0

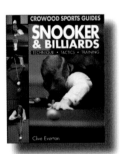

Snooker & Billiards
CLIVE EVERTON

ISBN 978 1 85223 480 5

Swimming
JOHN LYNN

ISBN 978 1 86126 757 3

Table Tennis
JENNY HEATON

ISBN 978 1 84797 090 9

Triathlon
STEVE TREW

ISBN 978 1 84797 170 8

In case of difficulty in ordering, contact the Sales Office:

The Crowood Press Ltd
Ramsbury
Wiltshire
SN8 2HR
UK

Tel: 44 (0) 1672 520320
enquiries@crowood.com
www.crowood.com